SUPER COOL TECH

TECHNOLOGY · INVENTION · INNOVATION

CONTENTS

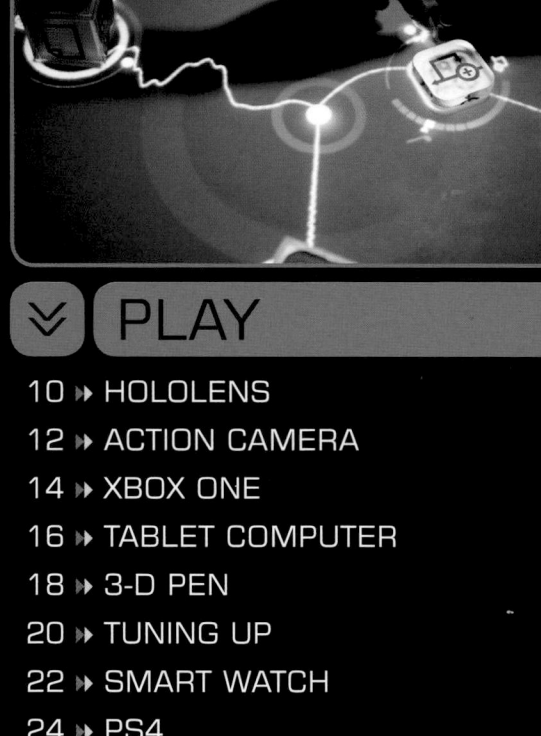

CONSTRUCT

POWER

⌄ FUTURE

⌄ LIVE

REFERENCE

 Penguin Random House

Art director Karen Self
Design director Phil Ormerod
Publishing director Jonathan Metcalf
Written by Ian Graham, Tom Jackson
Consultant Roger Bridgman

DK LONDON

Senior project editor Steven Carton
Senior art editor Smiljka Surla
Project art editor Laura Gardner
US editor Allison Singer
Managing editor Lisa Gillespie
Managing art editor Owen Peyton Jones
Producer, pre-production
Jacqueline Street
Producer Mary Slater
Jacket design development manager Sophia MTT
Jacket editor Claire Gell
Senior jacket designer Mark Cavanagh
Picture researchers
Steven Carton, Nic Dean
Publisher Andrew Macintyre
Associate publishing director
Liz Wheeler

DK DELHI

Project editor Antara Moitra
Project art editor Vikas Chauhan
Assistant editor Ateendriya Gupta
Art editors Sonali Rawat Sharma,
Mansi Agrawal
Assistant art editors Nidhi Rastogi, Priyanka
Bansal, Garima Sharma
DTP designers Sachin Gupta, Mohammad Rizwan
Senior DTP designer Harish Aggarwal
Picture researcher Deepak Negi
Managing jackets editor Saloni Singh
Pre-production manager Balwant Singh
Production manager Pankaj Sharma
Picture research manager
Taiyaba Khatoon
Managing editor Kingshuk Ghoshal
Managing art editor Govind Mittal

First American edition, 2016
Published in the United States
by DK Publishing
345 Hudson Street,
New York, New York 10014

Copyright © 2016 Dorling
Kindersley Limited

DK, a division of
Penguin Random House LLC
16 17 18 19 20 10 9 8 7 6 5 4 3 2 1

001—282971—September/2016

A catalog record for this book is available
from the Library of Congress.

ISBN 978-1-4654-5205-4

DK books are available at special discounts when
purchased in bulk for sales promotion, premiums,
fund-raising, or educational use. For details,
contact: DK Publishing Special Markets,
345 Hudson Street, New York, New York, 10014
SpecialSales@DK.com

Printed in China

A WORLD OF IDEAS:
SEE ALL THERE IS TO KNOW
www.dk.com

PLAY

Some of the coolest technology is the most fun technology. This chapter is packed with things that are designed for you to play around with in your free time. Explore how holographic headsets, pens that can draw in midair, and wafer-thin television screens work.

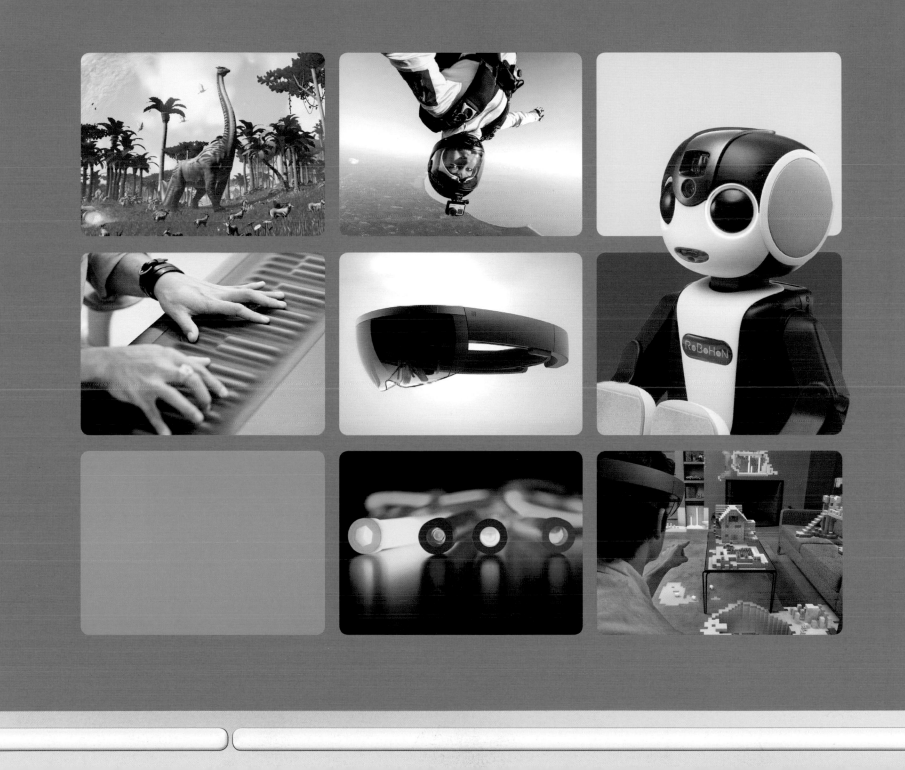

Play room

The HoloLens can transform any scene to suit any activity, such as playing a game. The device detects the shapes of the objects in the area and adds interactive holographic images to them wherever you look.

Holograms are placed over physical objects in the room.

Wearers can interact with the holograms using hand gestures.

HoloLens

▲ The HoloLens is a headset that allows you to view your surroundings through a transparent screen that also shows holographic imagery.

HOLOLENS

▶▶ The Microsoft HoloLens merges the real and virtual worlds through holographic technology. This is augmented reality, where physical objects have holograms laid over them. The HoloLens can turn any wall into a TV screen, turn any table into a personal computer, or create an entirely imaginary world to explore.

Head-mounted display

Pilots of the F35 Lightning II wear a head-mounted display that receives video feeds from cameras all around the aircraft. Using the display, the pilot can see right through the aircraft—just like wearing a pair of X-ray goggles.

F35 head-mounted display

Different uses

▶▶ The HoloLens can be used as a communication aid. A holographic video window shows the caller, but the technology also allows that caller to see the world just like you do—and even draw holographic instructions before your eyes.

Communication

Visualization

◀◀ The holographic processor is able to turn a 2-D design made on a screen into a 3-D version that can be viewed from all angles. The hologram can then be made real using a 3-D printer.

HOW IT WORKS

▶▶ The HoloLens contains three processors: One is the central controller, and another is for graphics, while the third scans the surroundings so holograms always appear in the correct places.

▲ Holograms can be manipulated by swiping, pinching, tapping, and rotating.

▲ HoloLens can be controlled with a large variety of simple voice commands.

▲ Sensors in the visor track the user's eyes and adjust the the holographic images to match.

▲ Holograms can be pinned in one place in the scene, so they behave as if they were physical objects.

▲ Holographic objects can also move around and interact with real objects in the scene.

▲ HoloLens can also create a scene that is completely filled with computer-generated imagery.

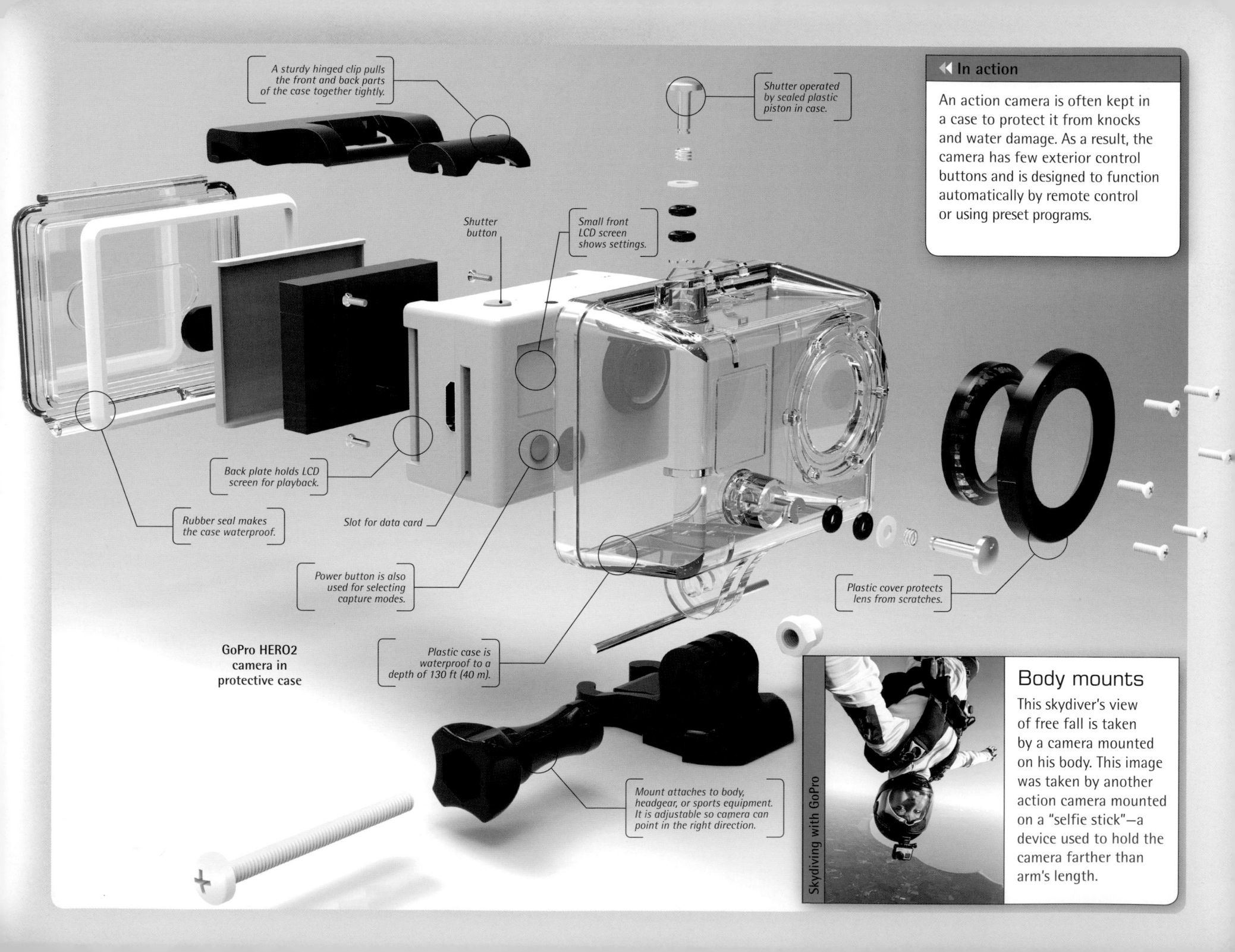

A sturdy hinged clip pulls the front and back parts of the case together tightly.

Shutter operated by sealed plastic piston in case.

Shutter button

Small front LCD screen shows settings.

Back plate holds LCD screen for playback.

Slot for data card

Rubber seal makes the case waterproof.

Power button is also used for selecting capture modes.

Plastic cover protects lens from scratches.

GoPro HERO2 camera in protective case

Plastic case is waterproof to a depth of 130 ft (40 m).

Mount attaches to body, headgear, or sports equipment. It is adjustable so camera can point in the right direction.

Skydiving with GoPro

Body mounts

This skydiver's view of free fall is taken by a camera mounted on his body. This image was taken by another action camera mounted on a "selfie stick"—a device used to hold the camera farther than arm's length.

ACTION CAMERA

▶▶ Digital cameras have changed the way we record our special memories. Small action cameras are tough enough to be taken anywhere, and also powerful enough to bring back a pin-sharp record of the most exciting action. The high-definition images show what it would be like if you were there, right in the action, doing it yourself.

HOW IT WORKS

▷▷ The GoPro HERO4 Session is one of the smallest action cameras. It is a 1.6-in (4-cm) cube that is fully waterproof without needing an extra case. Its small size and 2.6 oz (74 g) weight make it ideal for capturing even the most extreme action.

The camera's power button is on top.

Video and images from the camera can be synchronized wirelessly to an app.

The camera can be controlled by wireless devices.

A mount can be used to protect and steady the camera.

Smartphone

Tablet

Cool cameras

◀◀ In 2012, Felix Baumgartner flew a helium balloon to 127,850 ft (38,969 m) above the deserts of New Mexico— and then jumped out. Action cameras recorded every bit of this incredible journey, from the amazing high-altitude views of Earth to his free fall. The Austrian daredevil broadcast images live to the world as he became the first skydiver to break the sound barrier on his descent, before parachuting safely to the ground.

Cameras record Baumgartner's historic jump

▶▶ The Large Synoptic Survey Telescope is a 3.2-billion-pixel digital camera. Currently being built in the dry mountains of Chile, the device is designed to look for small objects in the solar system. It will require an array of 1,500 high-definition television screens to display a single full-size picture snapped by the camera.

Large Synoptic Survey Telescope

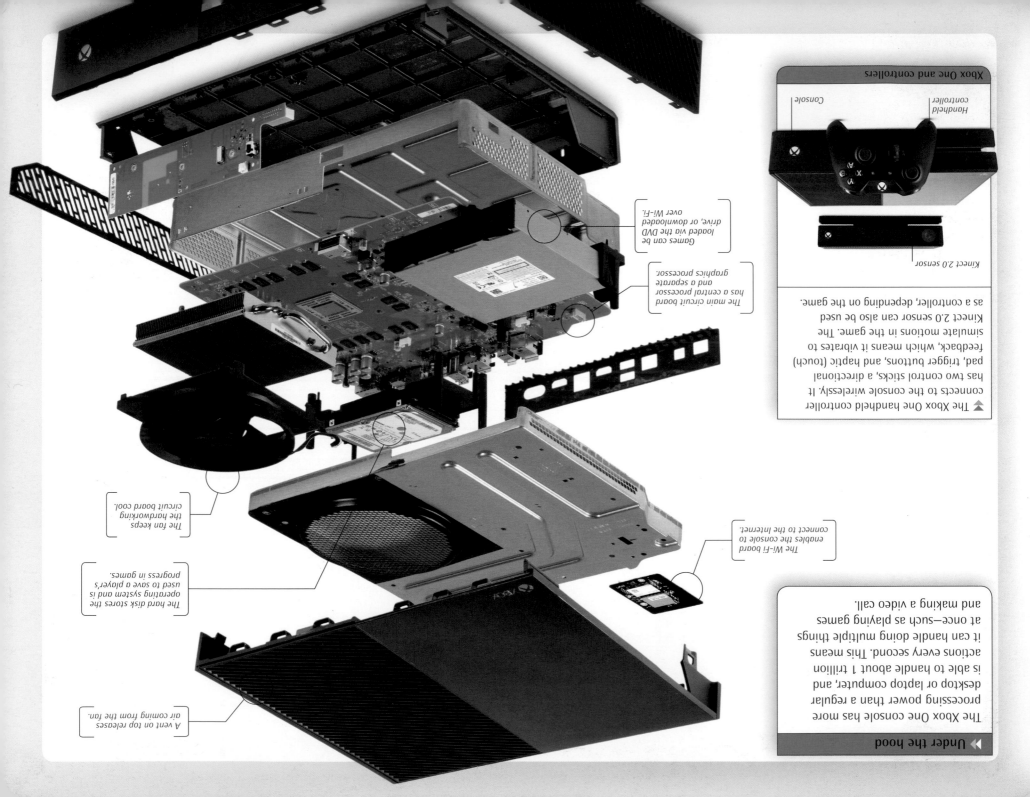

Handheld
controller

Console

Kinect 2.0 sensor

▲ The Xbox One handheld controller
connects to the console wirelessly. It
has two control sticks, a directional
pad, trigger buttons, and haptic (touch)
feedback, which means it vibrates to
simulate motions in the game. The
Kinect 2.0 sensor can also be used
as a controller, depending on the game.

Games can be
loaded via the DVD
drive, or downloaded
over Wi-Fi.

The main circuit board
has a central processor
and a separate
graphics processor.

The fan keeps
the hardworking
circuit board cool.

The hard disk stores the
operating system and is
used to save a player's
progress in games.

The Wi-Fi board
enables the console to
connect to the Internet.

A vent on top releases
air coming from the fan.

◀◀ Under the hood

The Xbox One console has more
processing power than a regular
desktop or laptop computer, and
is able to handle about 1 trillion
actions every second. This means
it can handle doing multiple things
at once—such as playing games
and making a video call.

XBOX ONE

▶▶ The Xbox One is one of the most powerful gaming consoles ever created. Its powerful processors are able to handle detailed and fast-moving graphics across an array of games. Most games are played using the handheld controller, but the console's incredibly sensitive Kinect 2.0 sensor allows the player's whole body to be used also. It's not just a gaming console, however; it can also be used as a communication and media center to keep in touch with friends through online video calls, and stream music and movies from the Internet.

Graphics from the game *Forza Motorsport 6*

Great graphics

The Xbox One's graphics are created by a GPU, or Graphics Processing Unit, which is a separate microchip to the main processor. This works with the large internal memory to produce complex, realistic graphics that move smoothly like a video and respond in real time to inputs from controllers.

⌄ KINECT 2.0 SENSOR

⤒ The Kinect 2.0 sensor is one of the most sensitive sensors available. It allows players to use body movements and voice commands to control games, but it is also able to monitor their heart rate, blood pressure, and eye movements.

⤒ Kinect is able to track the movements of six players at once, and so each player's body becomes a game controller. Games controlled in this way include sports simulation and multiplayer games, such as the one above.

⤒ The sensor uses an infrared camera to recognize a shape by bouncing an infrared beam off it to measure its distance from the console. It is able to pick out facial features in this way, so players can create their own avatars to take part in games.

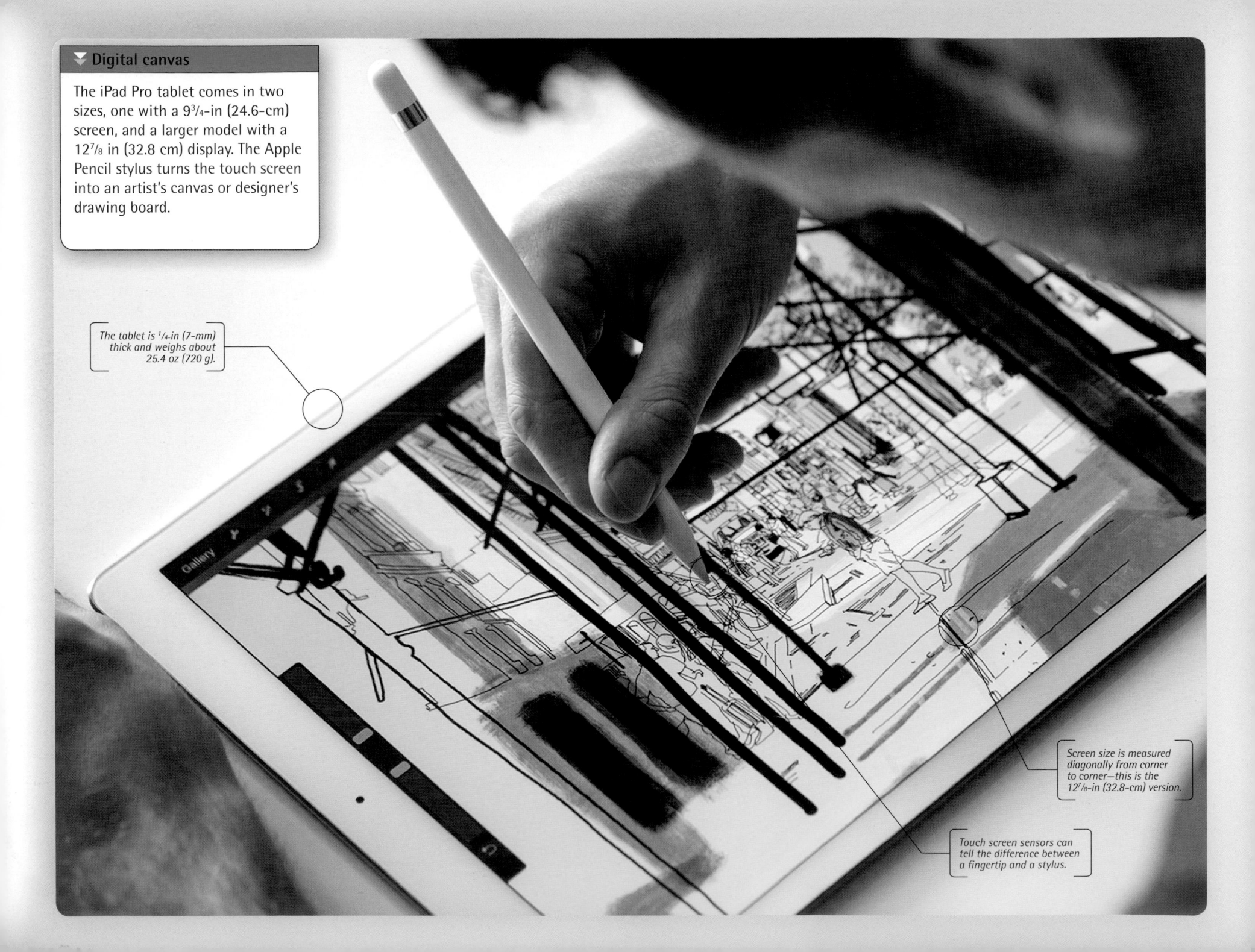

The tablet is ¼-in (7-mm) thick and weighs about 25.4 oz (720 g).

Screen size is measured diagonally from corner to corner—this is the 12⅞-in (32.8-cm) version.

Touch screen sensors can tell the difference between a fingertip and a stylus.

TABLET
COMPUTER

▶▶ Without a doubt, the biggest revolution in computing in recent years is the rise of the tablet computer. With the increasing power and decreasing size of computer components, it has been possible to pack a lot of processing power into a small frame. Computers have become smaller, more mobile, and easier to use than traditional desktop or laptop computers. Tablet computers like American company Apple's iPad Pro are designed to be light enough to be held easily, but also big and powerful enough to be used to create things, not just to view them.

The Apple Pencil

The weight and size of the Apple Pencil stylus matches that of a real pencil, and its tip sends data to the iPad display so it draws like a real pencil, too. The screen can detect when it is touched with the stylus tip and scans for contact twice as often—240 times a second—as it does with a fingertip. Pressure sensors in the tip detect the force applied to the stylus, which is translated into the thickness of the line created. The lightest touch can contact a single pixel on the screen. The stylus has two accelerometers, which detect the angle and orientation of the tip to create a shading effect.

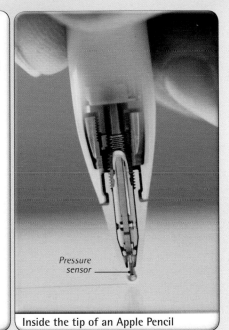

Pressure sensor

Inside the tip of an Apple Pencil

⌄ HOW IT WORKS

▶▶ The iPad Pro has two cameras (front and back), four speakers, and two microphones for playing and recording stereo sounds, and it can connect to wireless and mobile networks. However, its main component is the large touch screen, which has to be highly efficient so it doesn't drain the battery. It achieves this by adjusting the number of times the image displayed on screen is updated. When showing videos or games, the display is refreshed 60 times a second, so the eye sees a consistently moving image. However, when the display is of a static subject, the refresh rate is halved, saving valuable energy.

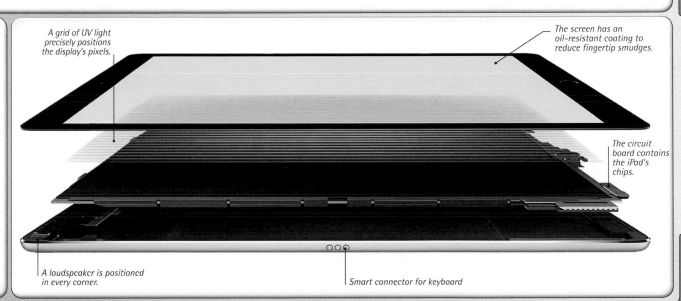

A grid of UV light precisely positions the display's pixels.

The screen has an oil-resistant coating to reduce fingertip smudges.

The circuit board contains the iPad's chips.

A loudspeaker is positioned in every corner.

Smart connector for keyboard

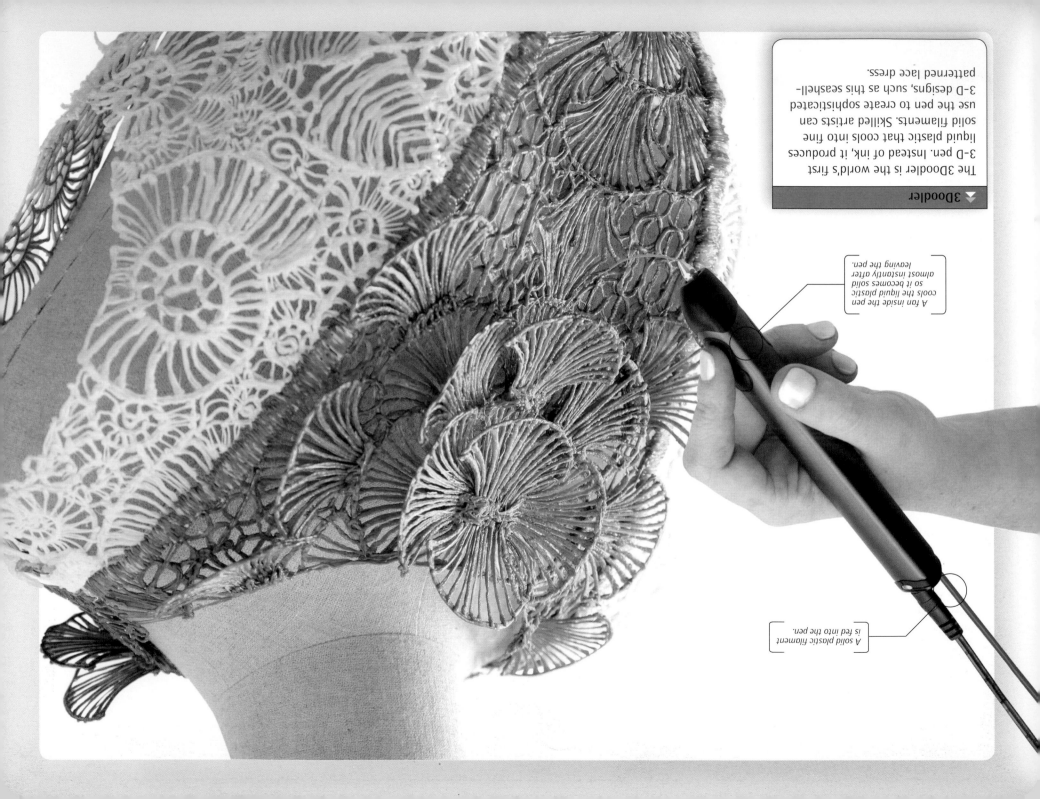

A fan inside the pen cools the liquid plastic so it becomes solid almost instantly after leaving the pen.

A solid plastic filament is fed into the pen.

3-D PEN

Though it may not look like it, the 3Doodler is the smallest 3-D printer in the world. The basic concept of the 3Doodler is an extension of the emergence of 3-D printing technology: Just as a 3-D printer uses droplets of quick-drying liquid plastic to produce solid structures, the 3Doodler pen does the same, but this handheld gadget does it on a smaller scale. Unlike a normal 3-D printer, however, the pen allows users to develop and change their designs as they go along.

Printing food

3-D printers are able to make almost anything you want, and they can make things out of materials other than plastic. The Bocusini system uses food as its material. It can produce intricate dishes from liquid chocolate and dairy products, as well as purees of vegetables and meat.

A marzipan printed cake decoration

HOW IT WORKS

A 3-D printer always follows a preset pattern, whereas a 3-D pen is a freehand device entirely controlled by the user. You can use it to create textured artwork on paper, but unlike a regular pen, you can also draw into the air. With practice and patience, a 3-D pen can be used to produce unique models and artworks, and even to draw replacement parts or mend broken components.

A flexible filament of the desired color is fed into the end of the pen. The filament is thermoplastic, meaning it will become soft and flexible when heated and retain its shape once it cools down.

The speed at which the plastic flows can be altered to create different effects. Unlike an ink pen, the plastic emerges even when the pen is held still.

Multicolored objects can be made by using different plastic filaments.

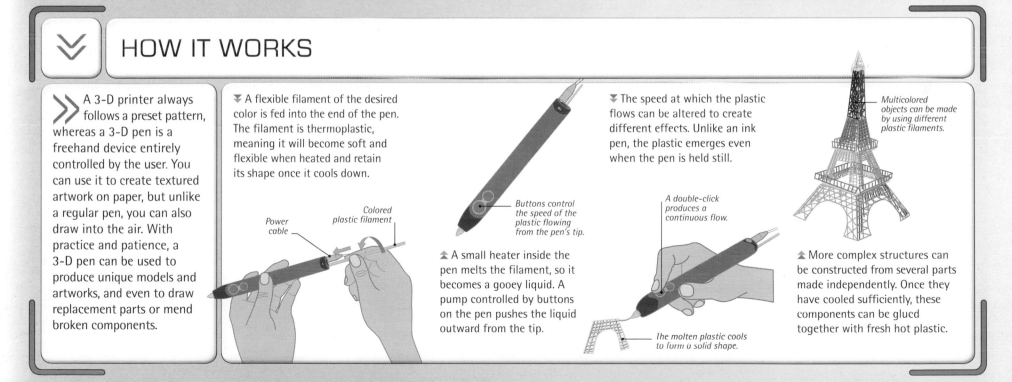

Power cable

Colored plastic filament

Buttons control the speed of the plastic flowing from the pen's tip.

A small heater inside the pen melts the filament, so it becomes a gooey liquid. A pump controlled by buttons on the pen pushes the liquid outward from the tip.

A double-click produces a continuous flow.

The molten plastic cools to form a solid shape.

More complex structures can be constructed from several parts made independently. Once they have cooled sufficiently, these components can be glued together with fresh hot plastic.

TUNING UP

Inspired designers are using revolutionary technology to develop a range of pretty cool new musical instruments. Some of these are based on traditional instruments like violins and pianos. Other technological advances are completely changing the way we play and listen to music.

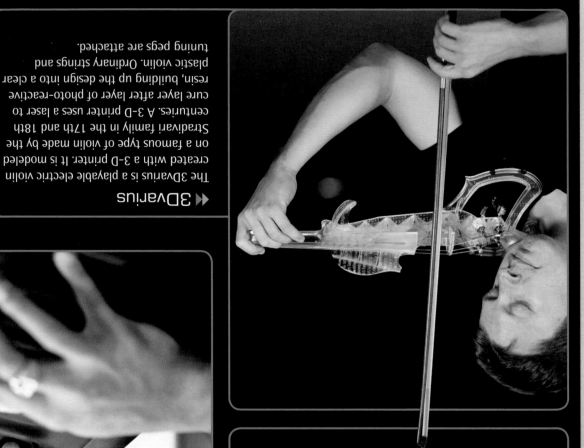

▶▶ 3Dvarius

The 3Dvarius is a playable electric violin created with a 3-D printer. It is modeled on a famous type of violin made by the Stradivari family in the 17th and 18th centuries. A 3-D printer uses a laser to cure layer after layer of photo-reactive resin, building up the design into a clear plastic violin. Ordinary strings and tuning pegs are attached.

▶▶ Seaboard GRAND

ROLI's Seaboard GRAND is a reinvention of the piano. Its soft, touch-sensitive surface gives players more control over sound. They can bend the pitch by moving fingers rapidly from side to side, like vibrato on a violin or guitar, as well as deepen sounds by pressing into the silicone keys.

Here Active Listening

Annoying wires trailing from earphones could soon be a thing of the past. Earbuds made by Here Active Listening are completely wireless. They connect to a smartphone app that lets users control volume and filter out unwanted sounds. When not in use, the buds are stored in a case that works as a charger.

Silent Guitar

With Yamaha's Silent Guitar, musicians can play and practice as much as they want without disturbing the neighbors. Plugging in headphones gives the player full sound but the guitar can hardly be heard at all by anyone else. The guitar can be amplified for playing live, and it can be dismantled for traveling.

Reactable

The Reactable system is a computer-linked tabletop with an illuminated display of symbols. Users can create music and sound effects by placing objects called tangibles on the table. Different tangibles control different sounds, and interacting with their position on the table changes the sounds the system produces.

Watch features

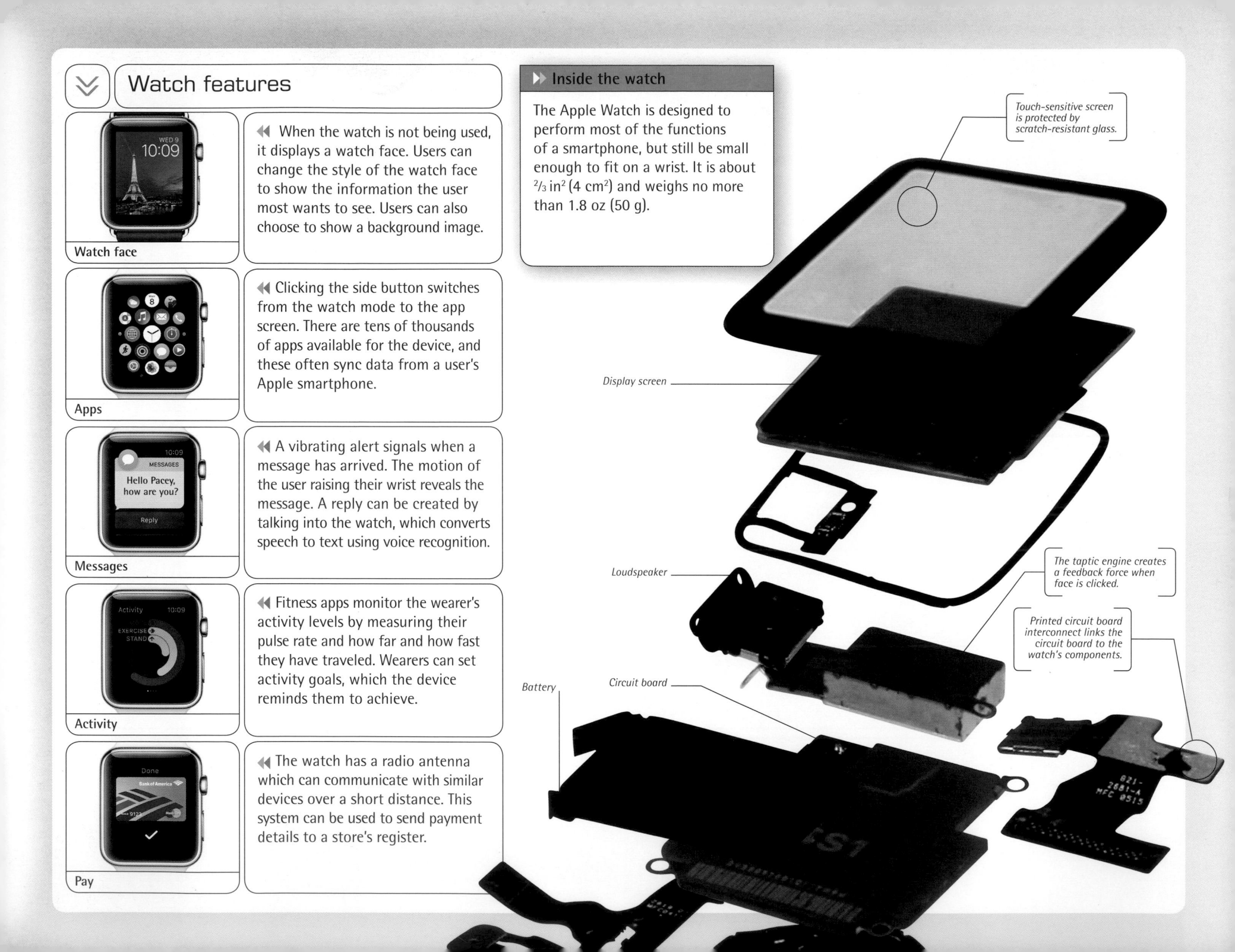

Watch face

◀◀ When the watch is not being used, it displays a watch face. Users can change the style of the watch face to show the information the user most wants to see. Users can also choose to show a background image.

Apps

◀◀ Clicking the side button switches from the watch mode to the app screen. There are tens of thousands of apps available for the device, and these often sync data from a user's Apple smartphone.

Messages

◀◀ A vibrating alert signals when a message has arrived. The motion of the user raising their wrist reveals the message. A reply can be created by talking into the watch, which converts speech to text using voice recognition.

Activity

◀◀ Fitness apps monitor the wearer's activity levels by measuring their pulse rate and how far and how fast they have traveled. Wearers can set activity goals, which the device reminds them to achieve.

Pay

◀◀ The watch has a radio antenna which can communicate with similar devices over a short distance. This system can be used to send payment details to a store's register.

▶▶ Inside the watch

The Apple Watch is designed to perform most of the functions of a smartphone, but still be small enough to fit on a wrist. It is about $2/3$ in^2 (4 cm^2) and weighs no more than 1.8 oz (50 g).

Touch-sensitive screen is protected by scratch-resistant glass.

Display screen

Loudspeaker

The taptic engine creates a feedback force when face is clicked.

Printed circuit board interconnect links the circuit board to the watch's components.

Battery

Circuit board

SMART WATCH

▶▶ As computer chips get smaller and more powerful, it has become possible for them to drive something as small as a wristwatch. The Apple Watch is an example of a "smart watch." It tells the time, but its computer makes it possible also to make and receive calls and messages, and use apps. The watch connects to the phone network and Internet.

The IBM WatchPad

WatchPad

The concept of the smart watch has been around for a while. This prototype WatchPad was released by American technology company IBM in 2001. It connected to the Internet and received emails and texts, but it had limited functions and a battery life of only a few hours.

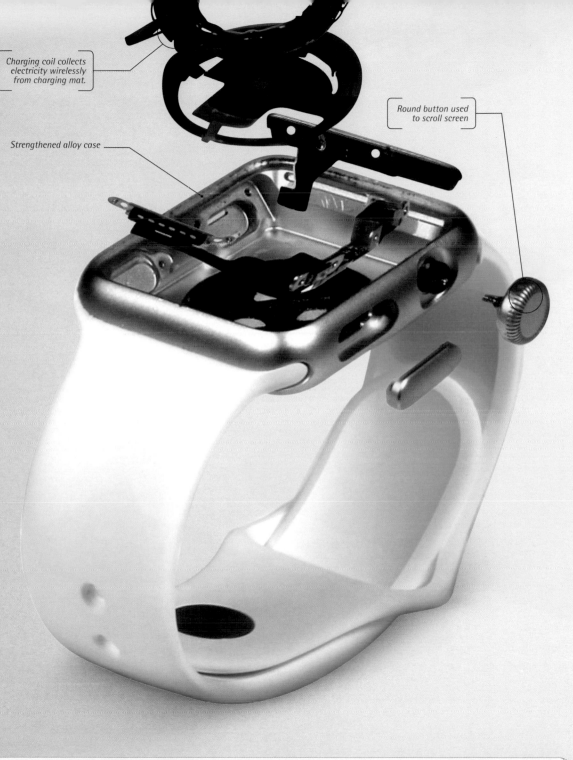

Charging coil collects electricity wirelessly from charging mat.

Round button used to scroll screen

Strengthened alloy case

DUALSHOCK

The PS4 DualShock controller has two joysticks, several trigger buttons, and a trackpad. It also contains accelerometers, which detect the motion of the controller so it can be used like a steering wheel. When more than one controller is connected to a console, the light bar on each one lights up in a different color, matching the player's character on screen.

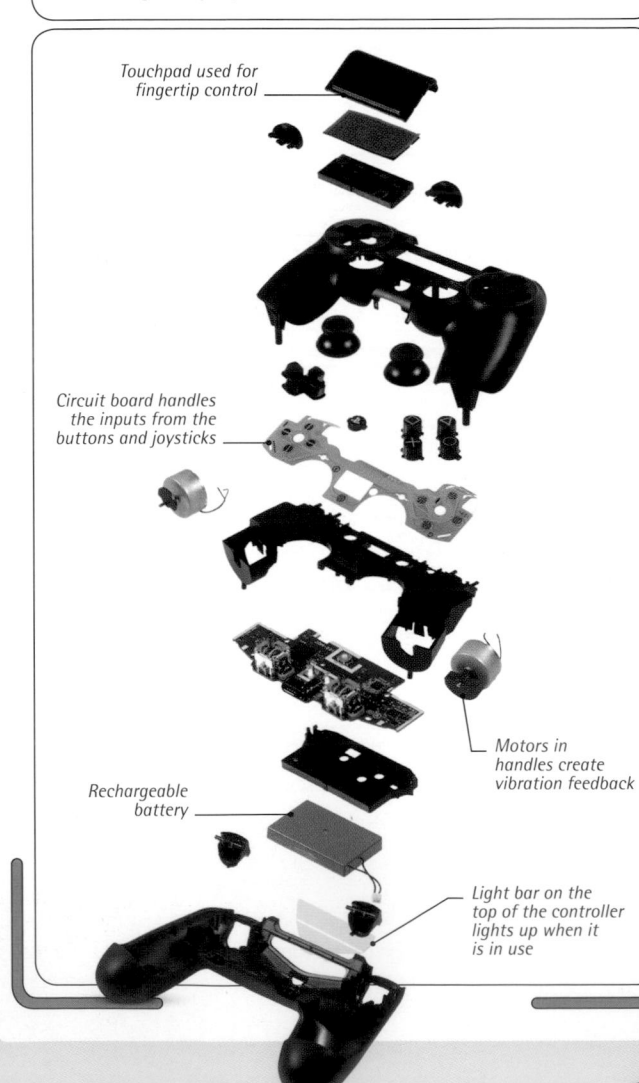

Touchpad used for fingertip control

Circuit board handles the inputs from the buttons and joysticks

Motors in handles create vibration feedback

Rechargeable battery

Light bar on the top of the controller lights up when it is in use

Under the hood

The PlayStation 4's internal hardware is similar to a home computer, which makes it easier for developers to make games for the console. The PS4 is able to carry out 1.8 trillion separate calculations every second.

Inside a PlayStation 4

A metal bracket protects the circuit board and hard drive underneath.

The hard drive stores games, the operating system, and game-save data.

A fan-assisted heat sink under the circuit board makes sure the electronics do not overheat.

PS4

The optical drive is used for loading games and playing DVDs and Blu-ray disks.

▶▶ Since its launch in late 2013, tens of millions of the PlayStation 4 (PS4) consoles have been bought by gamers across the world. It has become the most popular gaming console of recent years. Its popularity is largely based on the powerful technology inside its small frame—the PS4 offers the most impressive graphics and speed of any console currently available. Players can connect their smartphones to the console to play games on a mobile device, and a virtual-reality headset is due to be released in 2016.

The power supply keeps the console running.

Console and controller

The PS4 console is supplied with a wireless DualShock controller that connects using Bluetooth. There is also a motion-sensing system that works with the device, using two cameras to capture the position and movements of players and translating this into game play on screen. Players can also log in to the console by allowing the cameras to scan their face.

The console can be positioned horizontally or vertically, using a stand.

DualShock controllers come in a variety of colors.

PS4 and controller

No Man's Sky

No Man's Sky is a PS4 game that contains an entire, fictional universe. This computer universe is on the same scale as our own, containing 18 quintillion planets—or 18 million trillion. Players explore these planets, collecting resources and discovering what is there, and every planet has unique animals, weather, and landscape. The game designers did not plan each one—there are too many for that. Instead, they set up rules that govern the universe and allow the computer to create each planet as players arrive.

Alien life created in *No Man's Sky*

The display system is the depth of a credit card. It is light enough to be hung on the wall like a picture.

OLEDs create 16 million colors by combining red, green, and blue light produced by three kinds of chemicals.

◀◀ Curved screen

This TV produces a high-definition picture from a layer of OLEDs, or light-emitting diodes. That layer is 200 times thinner than a strand of hair, making an OLED screen flexible enough to be curved.

OLED TV

>> The future of television is here. TV manufacturers have tweaked traditional light-emitting diode (LED) TVs to add an organic (carbon-based) layer that produces colored light. The key to the technology is its carbon-based organic compound layer—traditional LED screens use several layers to make light and color, but the new OLED screens use only one. They produce images with better colors that change faster than LEDs. OLED TVs have thinner screens, use less energy, and are less polluting than other TVs.

HOW IT WORKS

>> An OLED display has pixels that are able to make a dot of any color by mixing red, blue, and green light. Each pixel contains three different OLED molecules that make light of one of these three colors. The quality of color images is improved because the OLEDs make only the exact colors required, and do not filter them from a white light source like other systems.

Flexi-tech

The screen of this flexible display contains a layer of OLEDs sandwiched between transparent plastic electrodes. It is flexible enough to bend or twist, and could even be rolled up. Flexible screens like this are being used in curved cell phones and tablets, where the screen wraps around the edge so messages can be displayed along the side of the device. Flexible OLED displays are even lightweight enough to be stitched onto fabric. As well as displays, OLEDs can produce light of a single color and be a highly versatile form of low-energy lighting that can be used just about anywhere.

A flexible OLED display

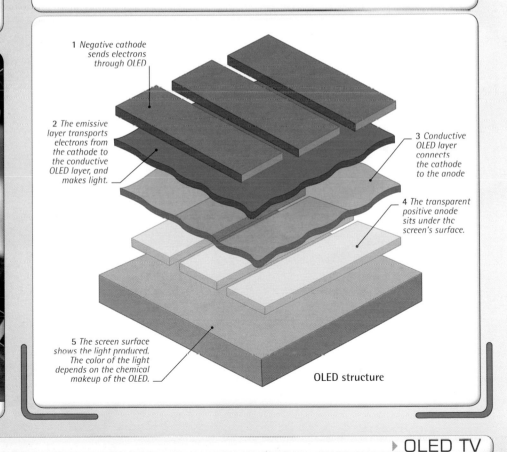

1 Negative cathode sends electrons through OLED

2 The emissive layer transports electrons from the cathode to the conductive OLED layer, and makes light.

3 Conductive OLED layer connects the cathode to the anode

4 The transparent positive anode sits under the screen's surface.

5 The screen surface shows the light produced. The color of the light depends on the chemical makeup of the OLED.

OLED structure

Played like a violin

Strummed like a guitar

Played like a cello

▶▶ Palette of sounds

The Instrument 1 has a pressure-sensitive surface that works on the same principles as a touch screen or touch pad. It can be plucked, strummed, and tapped to emulate the keys, strings, and bowing action of several traditional instruments.

INSTRUMENT 1

▶▶ The basic designs of musical instruments haven't altered in hundreds of years, but technology is now changing all of that. The Artiphon Instrument 1 is a guitar, piano, violin, and drum machine all in one. It is designed to respond to the gestures a musician uses to play any of these instruments, and it can respond to different pressures for playing loud or soft, fast or slow. It can be played as a live instrument in the normal way, or used to record a sound symphony by connecting it to a computer.

⌄ HOW IT WORKS

▶▶ The Instrument 1 is played using a touch-sensitive fingerboard and six buttons on the bridge. If set in guitar mode, the bridge buttons are used for plucking and strumming, while touching the fingerboard alters the pitch. In piano mode, the fingerboard becomes a stacked six-octave keyboard, while for drumming, the fingerboard is divided into 12 pads.

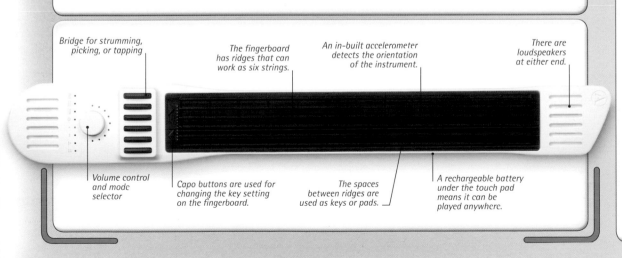

Bridge for strumming, picking, or tapping

The fingerboard has ridges that can work as six strings.

An in-built accelerometer detects the orientation of the instrument.

There are loudspeakers at either end.

Volume control and mode selector

Capo buttons are used for changing the key setting on the fingerboard.

The spaces between ridges are used as keys or pads.

A rechargeable battery under the touch pad means it can be played anywhere.

⌄ New sounds

Musical jellies

▲ French inventors have created a jelly-making kit that has a special twist: It can be used to make music. The colored, salty jellies are placed on a capacitor board that stores electrical energy. When you touch one of the jellies, it changes the electric field of the board, creating a sound that varies according to the shape, color, and saltiness of the jelly.

▶▶ Some instruments don't even need you to touch them to be able to play. The theremin was invented by Léon Theremin in 1928. It has two "antennas," which produce small electric fields. Moving your hands into a field alters its strength, which changes the sound given out by the machine. Moving closer to the tall antenna makes the note rise in pitch. Moving a hand away from the side antenna makes the sound louder.

Léon Theremin playing the theremin

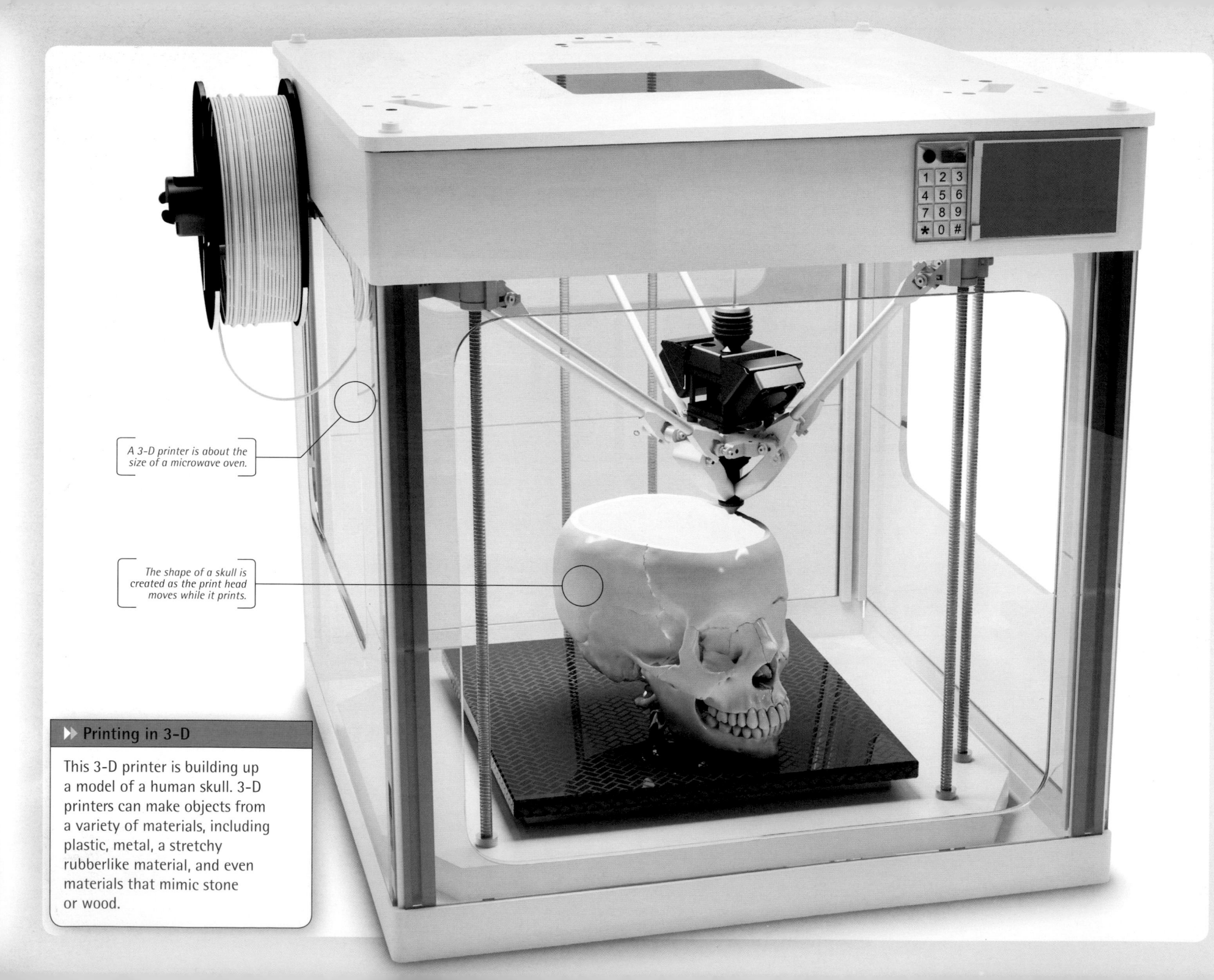

A 3-D printer is about the size of a microwave oven.

The shape of a skull is created as the print head moves while it prints.

▶▶ Printing in 3-D

This 3-D printer is building up a model of a human skull. 3-D printers can make objects from a variety of materials, including plastic, metal, a stretchy rubberlike material, and even materials that mimic stone or wood.

3-D PRINTER

▶▶ Traditionally, the process of making physical products was long, expensive, and difficult. It was often hard for designers, engineers, architects, and manufacturers to build, test, and refine their ideas. These days, however, it is possible for all of these professions to turn their ideas into reality by using a 3-D printer. It works just like a regular printer: A set of instructions is sent to the printer from a computer, and the printer turns these into a physical object. The latest 3-D printers can build complex shapes and even objects with moving parts. In future, they might be as inexpensive and as common as 2-D printers are now, making it possible for us to make many of the things we buy today.

HOW IT WORKS

▶▶ The printer melts a continuous filament of solid material and squeezes the liquid out through a fine nozzle onto a baseplate. The baseplate or the nozzle, or both, move according to a set of instructions to control where the liquid goes. When the first layer has been laid down, another layer is squeezed out on top of it. Then more layers are laid down, one by one, gradually building up the shape of a 3-D object.

3-D printing in space

The days when space station astronauts had to wait weeks or months for a tool or a replacement part to be sent up from Earth may be over. A 3-D printer was delivered to the International Space Station (ISS) in November 2014, enabling astronauts to make some of the things they needed. The printer was designed to work in the ISS's weightless environment. A few weeks after it arrived, the crew used it to make a socket wrench; the instructions for the tool were sent to the ISS printer from Earth, and it took four hours to make.

NASA's 3-D printer for use in space

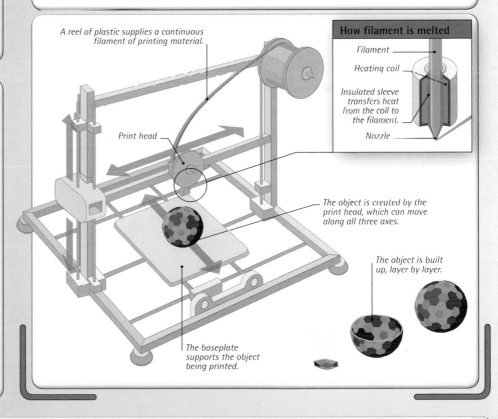

A reel of plastic supplies a continuous filament of printing material.

Print head

Print head

The object is created by the print head, which can move along all three axes.

The object is built up, layer by layer.

The baseplate supports the object being printed.

How filament is melted

Filament

Heating coil

Insulated sleeve transfers heat from the coil to the filament.

Nozzle

These football players have tiny radio tags in their uniforms. These provide real-time data about their locations and speeds, allowing fans to review and compare the latest performance statistics of their team's players.

Battery-powered tags the size of a coin are fitted inside the player's shoulder pads.

The tags send out a radio signal unique to each player.

RFID
TAGS

▶▶ Football is one of the latest sports to embrace radio-frequency identification (RFID) technology. RFID tags produce unique short-range radio signals that can identify and track any object or person. As well as being used to track athletes in sports events, RFID tags are used on many passports; to monitor books loaned out to people and returned to libraries; and on some debit, credit, and prepaid travel cards, for contactless payments.

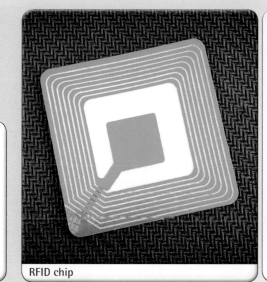
RFID chip

Passive tags
At 0.02 in (0.7 mm) thick, passive RFID tags are small enough to fit into credit cards and packaging. The tags have no power source, but they produce a weak radio signal when activated by a stronger radio wave from a tag-reading device. The tag's tiny ID signal can only be detected over a distance of about 2 in (5 cm).

⌄ HOW IT WORKS

Battery boosts the RFID tag's signal

Receiver

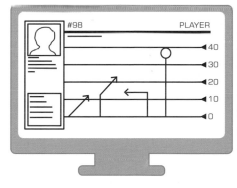
#98   PLAYER
40
30
20
10
0

⤒ Each player's tags broadcast ID signals 25 times a second. The signals are powerful enough to reach a loop of 20 radio receivers located around a field's edge.

⤒ The receivers pick up signals from all the tags on the field. The farther away a tag is from a receiver, the weaker the signal the receiver picks up. This information is used to calculate the exact location of each player.

⤒ The tags track the speed and direction of players at every step of the game. This makes it possible to compare the running speeds of defensive and offensive players as they compete for the ball.

⤒ The tag data from a game can be used to generate amazingly detailed performance statistics, such as how quickly players are able to change direction, their average jump height, and how often they stop to rest.

TECH TOYS

Toy designers are constantly coming up with amazing new ways of using advanced technology to create playthings for children. There is now a huge range of high-tech toys that are both fun and educational. They include robots that "know" their owners, Internet-linked toys, and interactive games.

◀◀ Code-a-Pillar

The Code-a-Pillar has eight segments that can slot together in any order. Each segment has an explanatory icon and controls one action, such as going forward or flashing lights. Once started, Code-a-Pillar performs a series of tasks in whatever order its segments are connected. By giving children lessons in sequencing, Code-a-Pillar can be seen as a first step in computer coding.

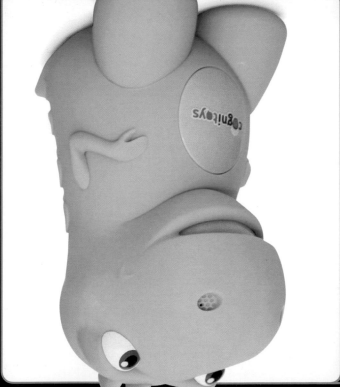

◀◀ CogniToys Dino

Dino is an Internet-linked dinosaur for children aged 5–9 that responds when spoken to. Children ask Dino questions (and get answers), give it commands, and interact with its jokes and stories. As a child gets smarter, so does Dino, matching the child's abilities in rhyming, math, spelling, and other skills.

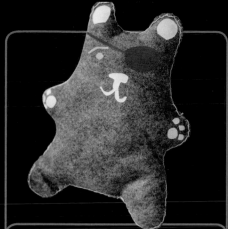

▼ Wondernik

These craft kits give children the challenge of making their own toys. Wondernik uses a range of different parts to teach children how things like motors, batteries, and switches work, and how to sew and draw. The kits include talking animals, a night-light house, and a wearable animal tail.

◀ Osmo

Combining physical tiles and an app, and a special scanner that fits over a tablet's front-facing camera, Osmo is a puzzle game with a twist. The app displays a puzzle, and the scanner lights up the tiles when they are put in the right places. Osmo comes with five games, including spelling, drawing, and number puzzles.

◀ RoBoHoN

Imagine a cell phone that's also a walking, talking, Web-connected robot that can recognize its owner's face and voice. RoBoHoN (from the Japanese words for robot and smartphone) is a cute little robot standing almost 8 in (20 cm) tall. It has a camera, an LCD screen, and a projector in its head.

Portable powerhouse

⯆ The screen can be folded over the keyboard to make a drawing surface. The stylus pen can be used to write or draw.

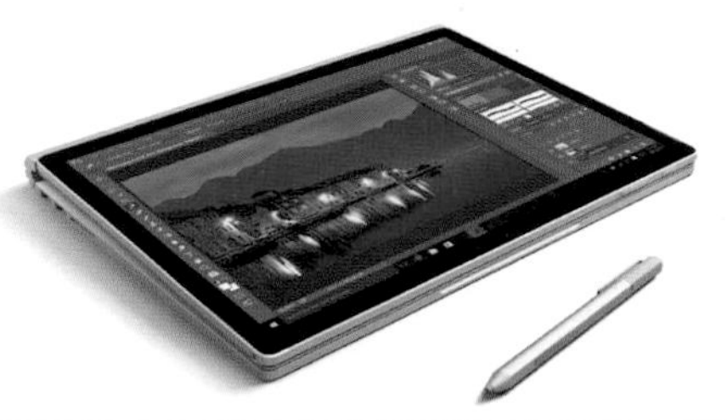

Canvas mode used for finely detailed work

⯆ The laptop is encased in magnesium, a tough but lightweight metal. The whole device weighs about $3\frac{1}{3}$ lb (1.5 kg) and is just under an inch (23-mm) thick when folded shut.

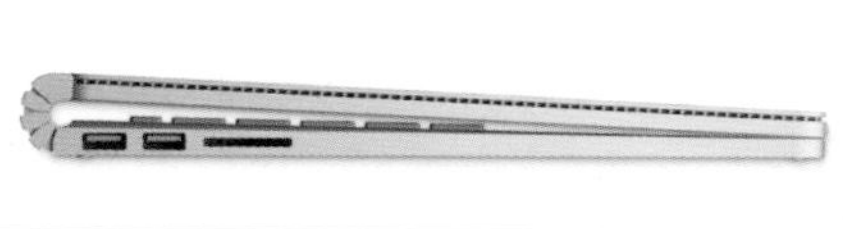

Surface Book from the side

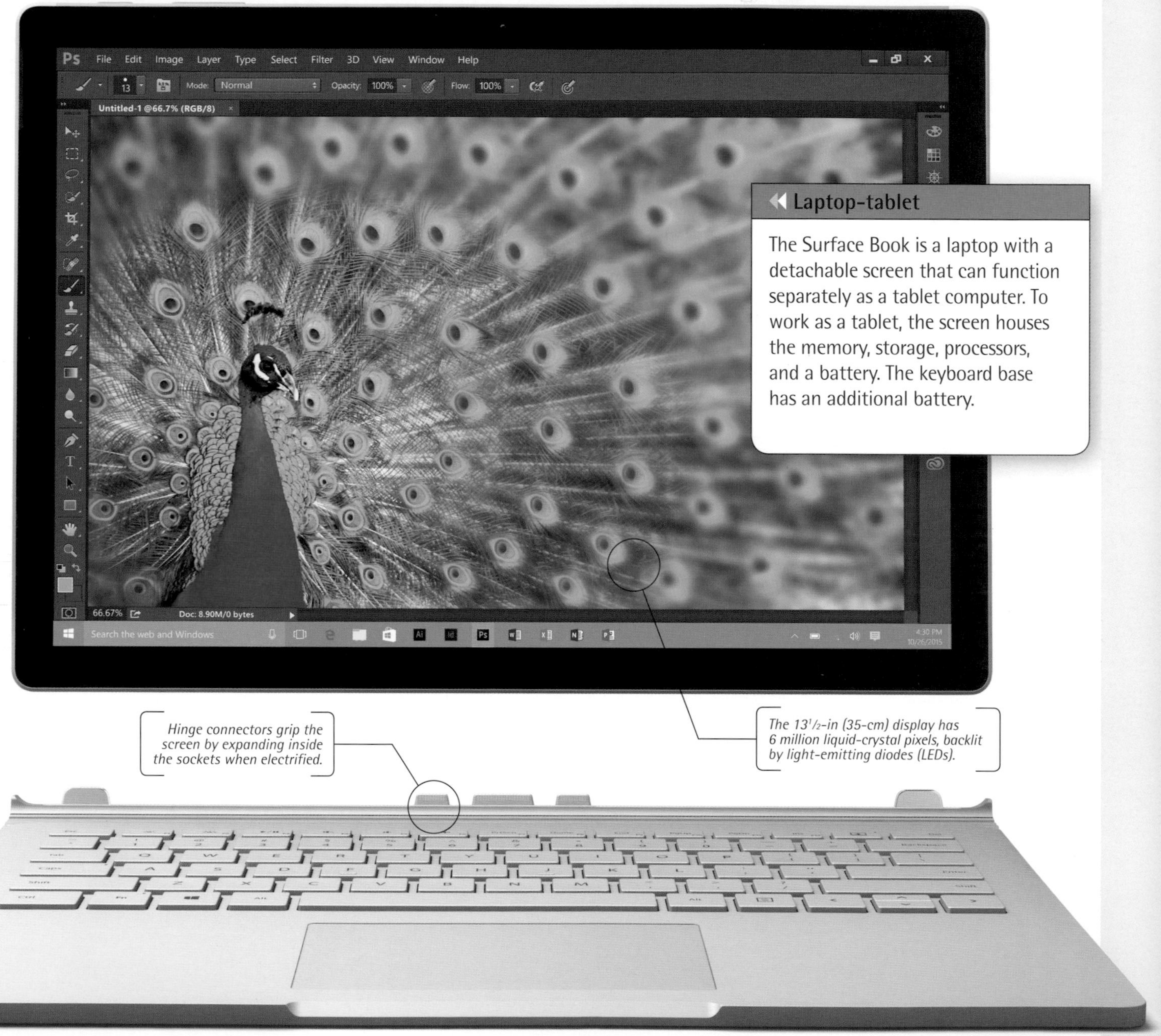

◀◀ Laptop-tablet

The Surface Book is a laptop with a detachable screen that can function separately as a tablet computer. To work as a tablet, the screen houses the memory, storage, processors, and a battery. The keyboard base has an additional battery.

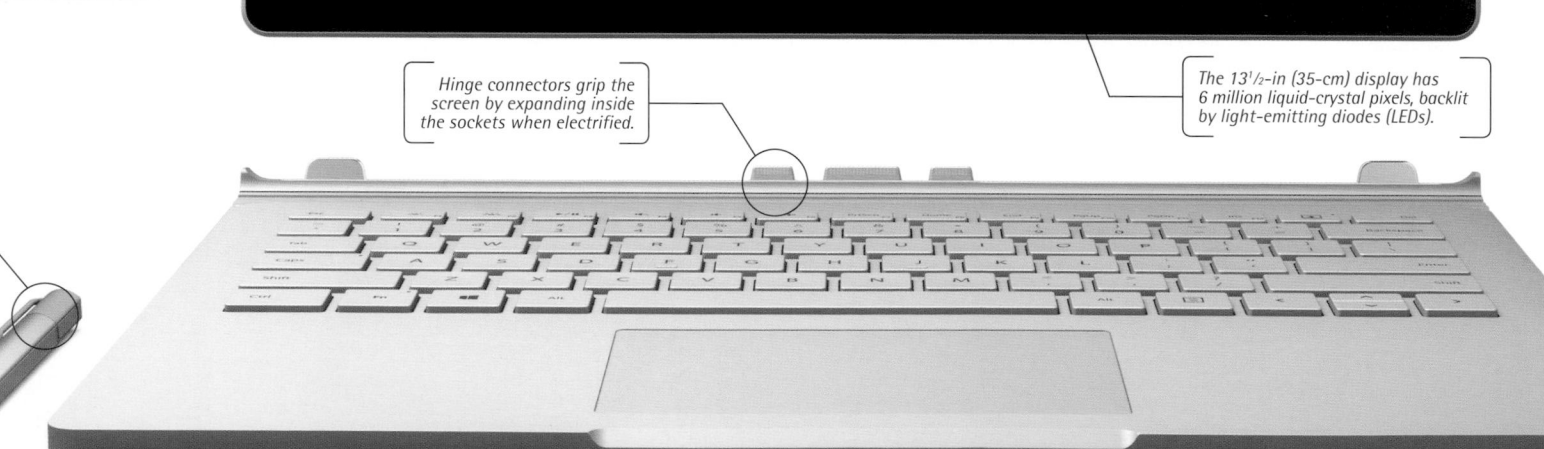

Hinge connectors grip the screen by expanding inside the sockets when electrified.

The $13\frac{1}{2}$-in (35-cm) display has 6 million liquid-crystal pixels, backlit by light-emitting diodes (LEDs).

A stylus pen can be used for drawing and navigation on the screen. It connects to the computer by Bluetooth.

SURFACE BOOK

▶▶ Able to work as a laptop, a tablet computer, or a touch-sensitive canvas, the Microsoft Surface Book shows how computers are changing to match the way we live and work. This fully portable and highly flexible gadget provides super-fast file transfer and a seamless experience in gaming, video editing, moviemaking, 2-D and 3-D rendering, and other graphics-intensive tasks.

⌄ HOW IT WORKS

▷▷ The touch screen detects a touch as a disturbance in a tiny electric field that covers its surface. When a finger (or pen) makes contact with the screen, some of the electric charge moves into the finger. To replace the charge lost from that part of the screen, tiny currents flow from power sources in the four corners. The processor in the computer is able to work out where the person is touching as a result.

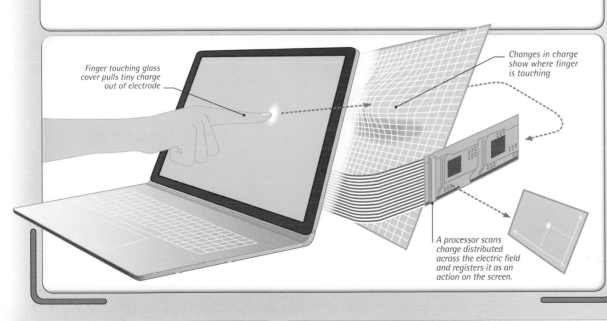

Finger touching glass cover pulls tiny charge out of electrode

Changes in charge show where finger is touching

A processor scans charge distributed across the electric field and registers it as an action on the screen.

⌄ Screen time

◀◀ The Surface Book has a liquid-crystal display (LCD), which shows images as colored dots. Light shines through minute dots called pixels, which each have a red, blue, and green filter. When liquid crystals are electrified, they block light from passing through particular filters in the pixel, creating images.

Liquid crystal display (LCD)

Osborne 1

▲ Laptops have come a long way since the Osborne 1, which was released in 1981. It weighed nearly 10 times as much as a Surface Book and was four times the price. Its main drawback, however, was its tiny 13 cm^2 (5 in^2) screen.

▲ Sticks of light and color

Once a glow stick is activated, it glows for as long as the chemical reaction inside it continues, and can't be reactivated afterward. The longest lasting glow sticks can keep glowing for up to 12 hours.

GLOW STICKS

▶▶ Glow sticks are responsible for the forest of brightly colored lights you regularly see at parties and pop concerts, but they also have more serious uses. They are often used for emergency lighting on trains and airplanes. Walkers, climbers, and sailors also carry them to signal to rescuers at night if they get into trouble. Glow sticks are popular light sources because they are inexpensive, they can be stored for long periods, and they can be activated quickly without any need for batteries or other power supplies.

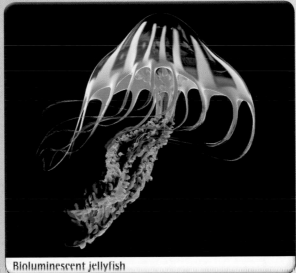

Bioluminescent jellyfish

Bioluminescence

Various organisms, like the jellyfish shown here, can make parts of their body glow by using chemical reactions similar to those used in glow sticks. The effect is called bioluminescence. Insects such as fireflies and glowworms use bioluminescence to attract mates or warn predators to stay clear. Some deep-sea fish have glowing lures that look like small creatures to attract prey.

⌄ HOW IT WORKS

▶▶ Glow sticks do not glow if they are not activated. To use one, you need to bend it, which breaks the small, brittle tube of hydrogen peroxide inside it. The outer tube is flexible and so does not break. When the hydrogen peroxide reacts with a chemical compound called diphenyl oxalate, energy is released. This is absorbed by a dye, which gives out the energy as colored light, with different dyes producing different colors.

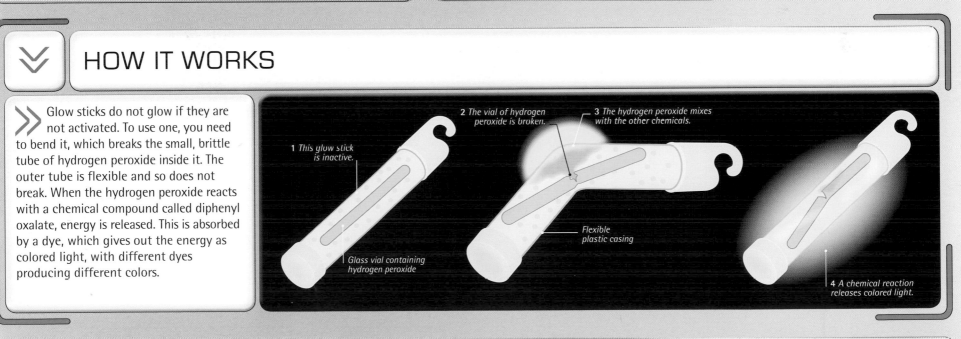

1 This glow stick is inactive.

Glass vial containing hydrogen peroxide

2 The vial of hydrogen peroxide is broken.

3 The hydrogen peroxide mixes with the other chemicals.

Flexible plastic casing

4 A chemical reaction releases colored light.

2

Since the first wheeled vehicles were built thousands of years ago, inventors have come up with lots of ways of moving faster and farther. These days, we are still finding new ways to go places. From hoverboards and giant cargo planes to super-rockets bound for other planets, there have never been so many options for getting around.

MOVE

The magnets in the base of the board are superconductors. To work, they have to be kept at −314°F (−192°C) by liquid nitrogen.

Supercooled nitrogen creates a fog

HOVERBOARD

▶▶ The hoverboard used to be pure science fiction. But in 2015, the Lexus Slide was unveiled in a one-of-a-kind "hoverpark" in Barcelona, Spain. The Slide makes use of the principle of magnetic levitation, and it took 18 months of research and development to make it so it was small and light enough to fit inside a skateboard.

Gliding on water

The Slide is pushed forward by the rider's kicks, like a normal board, but it is locked to the magnetism of the hoverpark's hidden track, gliding wherever that leads—even over water.

Hoverboard on a water-covered track

Shanghai Maglev Train

▶▶ The same principles of magnetic levitation used by the Slide are put to use in maglev trains, such as the Shanghai Maglev Train (SMT). As it floats frictionless above the ground, the train is pushed along at high speeds by a wave of magnetic forces running through the track.

Shanghai Maglev Train

14:33:58   428 km/h

Display showing the train's speed

◀◀ The SMT is the world's fastest passenger train. It makes the 18.6-mile (30-km) journey from Shanghai's central station to the airport in 7.3 minutes. Its maximum speed of 268 mph (431 kph) is faster than that of a Formula 1 race car.

HOW IT WORKS

▶▶ The Slide has a total of 32 supercooled superconductors hidden in its thick base. The magnetic forces from the track under the ground turn these conductors into powerful magnets, which push back with an equal force. The result is that the board and its rider are lifted off the ground. The board holds enough liquid nitrogen to levitate for 10 minutes before needing a refill.

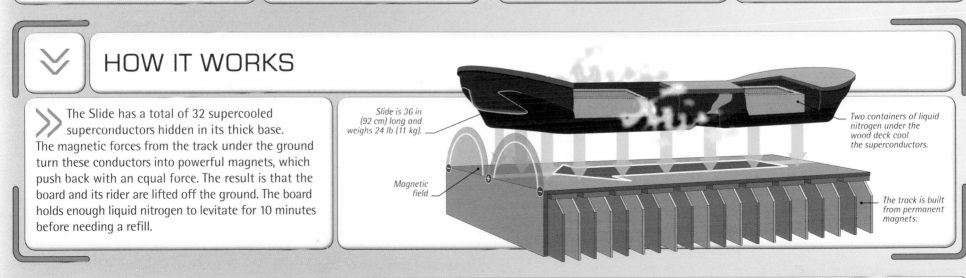

Slide is 36 in (92 cm) long and weighs 24 lb (11 kg).

Two containers of liquid nitrogen under the wood deck cool the superconductors.

Magnetic field

The track is built from permanent magnets.

Falcon Heavy is a two-stage rocket that stands 230 ft (70 m) tall. The first stage has three parts, or cores, each with nine identical rocket engines, making 27 engines in all. Each core is a Falcon 9, an earlier SpaceX rocket.

The second stage burns the same mixture of RP-1 fuel and liquid oxygen. It can be stopped and restarted to place payloads in different orbits.

A streamlined exterior houses the payload and protects it as the rocket travels through the atmosphere. It opens to release the payload.

Each of Falcon Heavy's three cores is a Falcon 9 rocket's first stage. The Falcon 9 is already in service.

Light and strong

▼ The thin walls of the Falcon Heavy's three first-stage cores and second stage are made of aluminum–lithium alloy. The addition of lithium makes the metal lighter and stronger than aluminum alone. The payload exterior is made of a lightweight composite material.

The 27 first-stage engines burn a mixture of RP-1 kerosene fuel and liquid oxygen. RP-1 is the same fuel used by jet airliners.

Inside the Falcon Heavy

SUPER ROCKET

▶▶ Falcon Heavy is the world's most powerful rocket. Built by American company SpaceX, it is designed to launch payloads (satellites or spacecraft) weighing up to 58 tons (53 metric tons) into space. When a Falcon Heavy rocket blasts off, its engines produce almost as much thrust as 18 jumbo jets, which is essential because the rocket needs to reach a speed of 25,000 mph (40,000 kph) to break free of Earth's gravity. Once free of Earth, the Falcon Heavy can be used to send astronauts to the moon, or perhaps to Mars.

Rocket capsule and booster

Cutting costs

Reusable rockets are set to become more common because they cut mission costs. An American company called Blue Origin is developing a wholly reusable rocket. In November 2015, the company successfully brought one of its rockets down to a controlled landing after a suborbital test flight.

HOW IT WORKS

▶▶ Most rockets are used only once and break up as they fall back to Earth. Falcon Heavy is designed to be partly reusable. It has three cores that return to Earth and land. Falcon 9 rockets have already tested this landing system. Following several failures, the core of a Falcon 9 landed successfully after launching a satellite in December 2015, and the first Falcon Heavy rocket is due to launch by 2017.

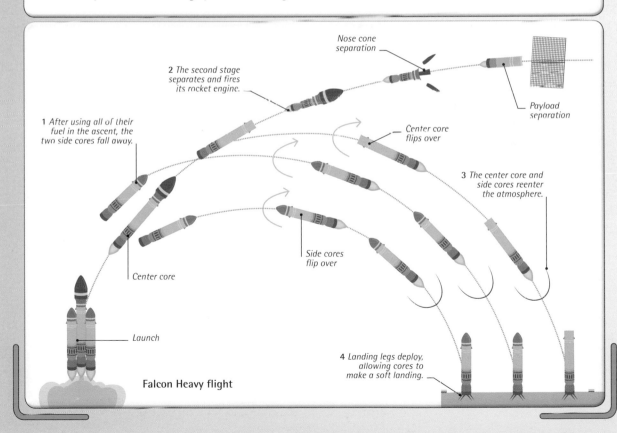

2 The second stage separates and fires its rocket engine.

Nose cone separation

Payload separation

1 After using all of their fuel in the ascent, the two side cores fall away.

Center core flips over

3 The center core and side cores reenter the atmosphere.

Center core

Side cores flip over

Launch

4 Landing legs deploy, allowing cores to make a soft landing.

Falcon Heavy flight

Mobility devices are often large, awkward to steer, and rarely great to look at. WHILL's designers want to change this image. Their device combines top performance and ease of use with a streamlined, futuristic design.

Innovative design

⬆ WHILL's unique front wheels ride easily over bumps, dips, and other small obstacles that get in the way. They also have a good grip on all surfaces, even on loose gravel or snow.

WHILL

▶▶ For the 100 million wheelchair users worldwide, the everyday world can be a hard place to get around. The WHILL personal mobility device is a new advance in technology that could make the many difficulties they face things of the past. This sleek power chair, which combines a hefty four-wheel drive (4WD) design with all-directional wheels, is designed for precision control on almost any type of terrain.

HOW IT WORKS

▶▶ What makes WHILL so different is the design of the two front wheels. These all-directional wheels run forward smoothly, but they can also get WHILL out of a tight corner. When turning space is limited, 24 small rollers around the edge of each wheel can steer WHILL in any direction, even sideways, or spin the chair around on the spot.

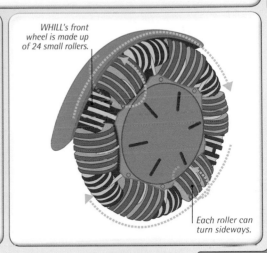

WHILL's front wheel is made up of 24 small rollers.

Each roller can turn sideways.

Key features

Using the app to control WHILL

Adjusts to suit the user

Easy-to-reach controls

Scalevo climbing stairs

⏶ The WHILL mobility device can be controlled remotely by a smartphone app. This also lets the user adjust the seat, alter the driving and control settings, and operate a security locking mechanism.

⏶ The seat can slide forward to let the user get into and out of the chair more easily. The positions of the seat back, arms, and footrest are also adjustable to suit users of different heights and mobility.

⏶ There is a mouse-like drive control on one handrest, and a switch for adjusting speed on the other. WHILL can travel up to 12 miles (19 km) on a single battery charge and has a top speed of 5.5 mph (8.8 kph).

Scalevo

Most wheelchairs are unable to climb stairs—but the Scalevo can. On level ground, it acts much like a regular wheelchair, but to climb stairs, it extends a pair of tank-like tracks, and goes up at the rate of one step per second.

▼ Clever car

The Model S's sleek body is packed with smart systems. It can steer itself to stay within a lane, change lanes when you tap the turn signal, set its speed by reading road signs, park itself automatically, and brake or steer itself to avoid collisions.

ELECTRIC CAR

▶▶ The Tesla Model S looks like many other cars, but it represents an automotive revolution. The Model S is an all-electric car, meaning that instead of having a gas-guzzling engine, it is powered by an electric motor. It's no slouch, either. It can get from 0 to 60 mph (100 kph) in as little as three seconds and reach a top speed of 155 mph (250 kph). Because the Model S doesn't burn any fuel, it doesn't give out any of the harmful greenhouse gases and sooty particles that pollute the environment, doing its bit to lessen our dependence on fossil fuels.

⌄ Car components

▶▶ The empty engine bay at the front of the car and the absence of a gas tank at the back provide extra storage space. This increases the total storage space of the car by almost 20 percent. It also makes the car easier to handle, since there is less weight in the front.

Front trunk

Plugging in to recharge

◀◀ The car's battery can be recharged from any electrical outlet. The charging port opens automatically when the car detects someone approaching with the charging connector. Special chargers are available that can charge half of the battery in 20 minutes.

⌄ HOW IT WORKS

The Tesla Model S has an advanced electric power train that is simpler, lighter, and more efficient than the equivalent system in a conventional car. When the driver presses the accelerator pedal, more electric current flows to the motor that turns the wheels. The motor is also used to slow the car by a process called regenerative braking. This converts the car's kinetic (movement) energy into electrical energy, which is stored in the battery. Most of the car's other functions are controlled via a 17-in (43-cm) tablet-like touch screen.

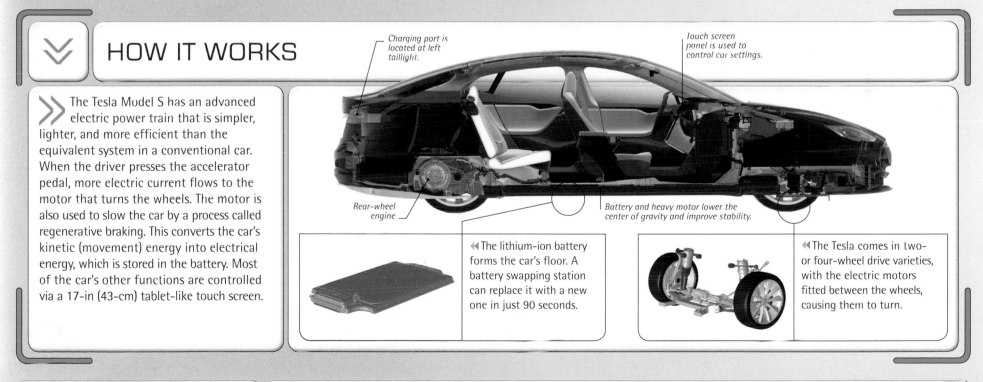

Charging port is located at left taillight.

Touch screen panel is used to control car settings.

Rear-wheel engine

Battery and heavy motor lower the center of gravity and improve stability.

◀◀ The lithium-ion battery forms the car's floor. A battery swapping station can replace it with a new one in just 90 seconds.

◀◀ The Tesla comes in two- or four-wheel drive varieties, with the electric motors fitted between the wheels, causing them to turn.

SpaceShipTwo's passengers can enjoy experiencing up to six minutes of weightlessness. They will be allowed to leave their seats and float about their cabin before strapping in again for reentry to Earth's atmosphere and landing.

A passenger on a test flight floats weightlessly inside SpaceShipTwo.

SPACESHIPTWO

▶▶ Within a few years, regular citizens could be experiencing the zero-gravity conditions of space on board a specially designed airplane called SpaceShipTwo. This rocket-powered craft is designed to carry ticketed passengers about 62 miles (100 km) into Earth's atmosphere, where space begins, and return them within three hours. The craft can reach the top speed of 2,500 mph (4,000 kph) that's necessary to break the bonds of Earth's gravity. If the craft's testing continues to be successful, there are plans for a fleet of five spaceplanes to be operated by Virgin Galactic from the purpose-built Spaceport America, in New Mexico.

Dennis Tito

Space tourism

SpaceShipTwo is still waiting to carry day-trippers, but space tourism is already here. The first space tourist was American millionaire Dennis Tito. In 2001, he paid $20 million to spend 7 days, 22 hours, and 4 minutes on board the International Space Station (ISS). He orbited Earth 128 times during his time in space.

⌄ HOW IT WORKS

▶▶ A SpaceShipTwo flight lasts about two and a half hours. A jet aircraft, WhiteKnightTwo, takes off carrying SpaceShipTwo. SpaceShipTwo falls away from the jet at 50,000 ft (15,000 m). It fires its rocket and climbs to 68 miles (110 km), crossing the boundary between Earth's atmosphere and space, where passengers experience weightlessness. After six minutes, it begins its descent, and at 15 miles (24 km) above Earth it prepares for landing.

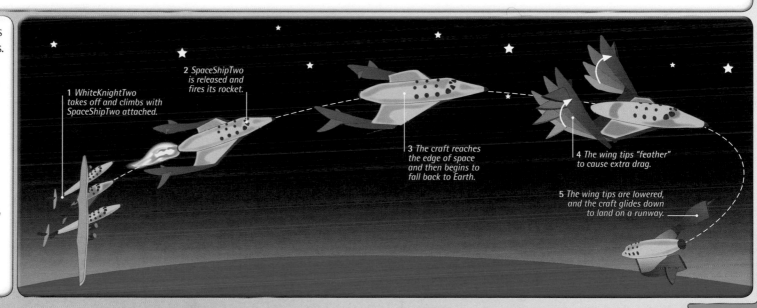

1 WhiteKnightTwo takes off and climbs with SpaceShipTwo attached.

2 SpaceShipTwo is released and fires its rocket.

3 The craft reaches the edge of space and then begins to fall back to Earth.

4 The wing tips "feather" to cause extra drag.

5 The wing tips are lowered, and the craft glides down to land on a runway.

Powered by waste

The Bio-Bus runs a regular public transportation service through Bristol, UK, powered by human sewage and food waste. After being processed at a biogas plant, these rotting materials become a super-clean, odor-free, low-carbon fuel.

The gas fuel is stored in a streamlined tank on the roof, compressed to 200 times the air pressure in the atmosphere.

This GENeco Bio-Bus is powered by your waste for a sustainable future **GENeco** Sustainable Solutions

Tell us what you think #biobus

The 40-seater bus can travel 186 miles (300 km) on a full tank of biogas.

The exhaust emissions contain 97 percent less smoke and 90 percent less nitrogen oxide than diesel-powered buses.

BIO-BUS

>> Unlike an ordinary bus, the Bio-Bus has an unusual power supply: human poo. Human waste from sewers can be collected and turned into biomethane, a highly flammable fuel. Because the raw ingredients of biomethane are both plentiful and completely renewable, the Bio-Bus shows us that clean fuel made in this way could one day be used to power our cars, heat our homes, and generate electricity.

HOW IT WORKS

Biomethane is made by heating waste inside tanks where all the air has been removed. Inside, bacteria turn the poo into biogas, which is 60 percent methane. Dust, bugs, and bad smells are filtered, and the biogas is then refined so it is 98 percent methane, which can be used as fuel for vehicles, or even supplied to homes.

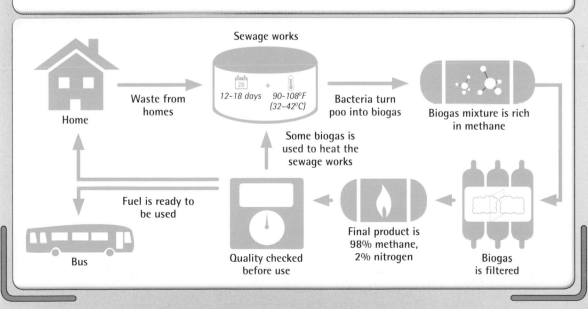

Home
Waste from homes

Sewage works
28
12-18 days + 90-108°F (32-42°C)

Bacteria turn poo into biogas

Biogas mixture is rich in methane

Some biogas is used to heat the sewage works

Fuel is ready to be used

Bus

Quality checked before use

Final product is 98% methane, 2% nitrogen

Biogas is filtered

A bioreactor grows oil-rich algae

⬆ One new source of oil fuel can be made with light. Tiny, plantlike algae use a source of bright light to grow inside an algal bioreactor, where they are kept free of impurities. The oils stored in the algae's cells are then refined into a fuel.

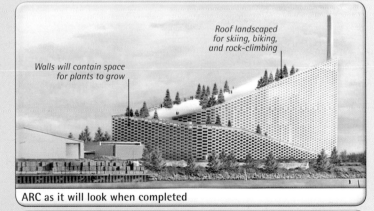

Roof landscaped for skiing, biking, and rock-climbing

Walls will contain space for plants to grow

ARC as it will look when completed

⬆ The trash cans of Copenhagen, Denmark, will become a source of power once the Amager Resource Center (ARC) is finished. This giant incinerator will make electricity from the heat of burning garbage. The vast building's sloping roof will also double as a ski run!

▶▶ Standing room only

ElliptiGO combines an elliptical machine, or cross-trainer, with a bicycle. Instead of sitting down and turning pedals, as on a normal bike, the rider stands up and uses a running action, as if using an elliptical machine in a gym.

The higher riding position makes it easier for the rider to see and be seen by other road users.

The handlebars are higher than on a normal bike to suit the rider's standing position.

Riding an ElliptiGO in a standing position burns 33 percent more calories than riding a conventional bike.

The rider stands on large platforms that support the rider's weight.

ELLIPTIGO

ELLIPTIGO

The ElliptiGO combines running and cycling in a unique machine. It's the brainchild of Bryan Pate, an American former athlete who was unable to run after suffering hip and knee injuries. Cycling is gentler on the joints than running, but can lead to neck and back pain. By combining the two in the ElliptiGO, users burn 33 percent more calories, but avoid many of the potential stresses and strains of either exercise.

Cardboard bike

Bizarre bikes

Bikes have been made of all sorts of materials, including cardboard and even grass. The cardboard bike is glued together and treated to make it waterproof and fireproof. The grass bike is made from a famously strong type of bamboo. These bikes are becoming more popular because they are inexpensive and environment-friendly.

HOW IT WORKS

ElliptiGO foot platforms and drive arms are designed to produce the same smooth elliptical foot motion as an elliptical machine. There are various models, with different stride lengths and stride heights to suit different users. A workout on an ElliptiGO uses the same muscles as running, but without the impact of feet pounding the ground, so it's equally suitable for leisure riders, athletes recovering from injuries, and aging riders with aching joints.

Gearwheel

▲ The rider starts by pushing down with one foot and forward with the other.

Drive arms

▲ The foot platforms move drive arms that turn the main gearwheel.

Drive chain

▲ The main gearwheel turns the rear wheel via a drive chain. An experienced rider can reach speeds of 20 mph (30 kph) or more.

▼ Multipurpose crew vehicle

Four astronauts in full launch suits test out the Orion's control array in a prototype crew module. NASA is developing Orion to carry human crews, first to the International Space Station, then to the moon, and possibly even to Mars.

Orion powered by four solar arrays

ORION

The Orion spacecraft is the next step in human space exploration, designed to take crews into deep space for the first time since the last Apollo moon mission in 1972. The spacecraft draws on engineering developed over the 50-year-long Space Race, and it makes use of design concepts from the Apollo project, the Space Shuttle launch system, and life-support technology used on space stations.

SLS flight concept

Space Launch System

A new launch rocket is being developed to carry Orion into space. Known as the Space Launch System (SLS), it will be the most powerful rocket ever built, capable of lifting at least 77 tons (70 metric tons)—the weight of 13 African elephants—into orbit. The main rocket will have four engines of the same design used by the Space Shuttle. Two solid-fueled rocket boosters will add to the thrust. The first SLS launch is planned for 2018.

HOW IT WORKS

Orion is made up of modules, which have specific functions. Four astronauts travel inside the pressurized crew module, while the service module behind holds the main rocket engine and the guidance jets used to steer in space. Both modules are launched on top of a rocket, but when returning to Earth, the crew module breaks off and is the only part that reenters the atmosphere.

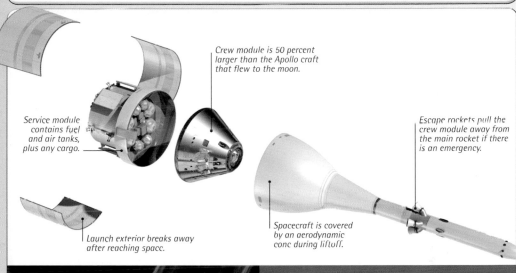

Crew module is 50 percent larger than the Apollo craft that flew to the moon.

Service module contains fuel and air tanks, plus any cargo.

Escape rockets pull the crew module away from the main rocket if there is an emergency.

Launch exterior breaks away after reaching space.

Spacecraft is covered by an aerodynamic cone during liftoff.

Heat shield protects crew module during reentry

Module parachutes to an ocean splashdown

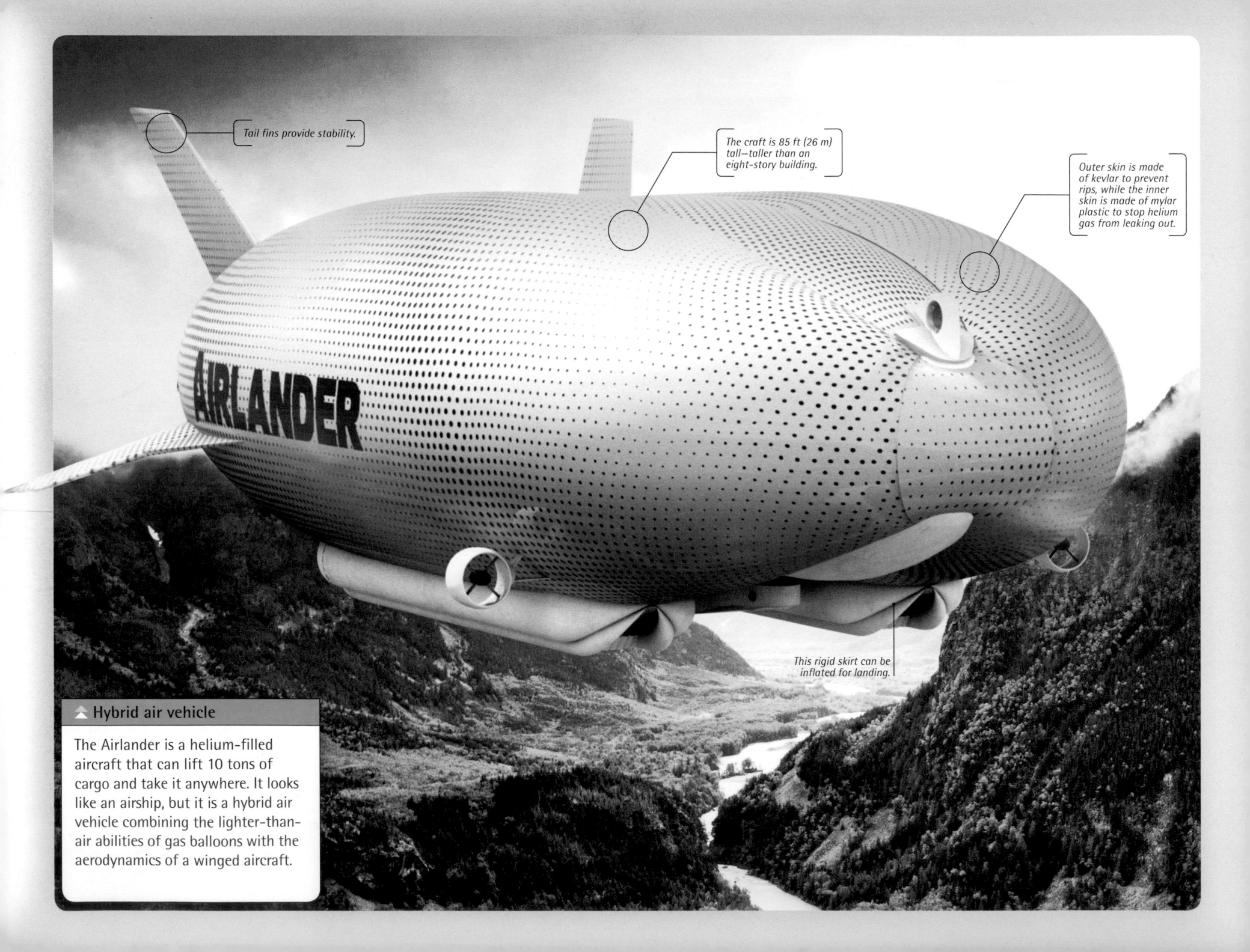

Tail fins provide stability.

The craft is 85 ft (26 m) tall—taller than an eight-story building.

Outer skin is made of kevlar to prevent rips, while the inner skin is made of mylar plastic to stop helium gas from leaking out.

AIRLANDER

This rigid skirt can be inflated for landing.

⏶ Hybrid air vehicle

The Airlander is a helium-filled aircraft that can lift 10 tons of cargo and take it anywhere. It looks like an airship, but it is a hybrid air vehicle combining the lighter-than-air abilities of gas balloons with the aerodynamics of a winged aircraft.

AIRLANDER

▶▶ The Airlander is the largest aircraft ever to have flown. It is 302 ft (92 m) long and has a total volume of 1,340,000 ft³ (38,000 m³). It can fly at 9,840 ft (3,000 m) and cruise at a speed of 92 mph (148 kph), staying aloft for five days—longer if it is remotely controlled from the ground. The vast aircraft uses three distinct ways of staying in the air: Most lift comes from the buoyancy of the lighter-than-air helium gas; further lift is created by the wing shape of the three gas-filled hulls; and more force is added by the propeller-powered thrusters, which can be angled in any direction.

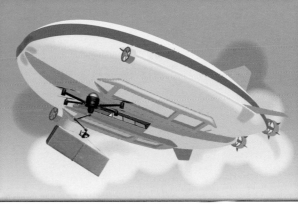
A delivery drone coming from the Airlander

Cargo carrier

The Airlander is a very versatile aircraft: It can take off and land without a runway, hover in the air, and access remote places, carrying heavy cargos far beyond the capacity of other craft. It could be used as an airborne mothership for delivery drones, which can't fly very far or for very long without needing to be refueled.

HOW IT WORKS

▶▶ At sea level, the hull of the Airlander holds mostly helium gas with air inside small ballonets. As the aircraft rises, the atmospheric pressure outside falls, and the helium gas expands. Air escapes from the ballonets, reducing the aircraft's weight. To reduce altitude, the helium is compressed into storage tanks, which allows air back inside, increasing the aircraft's weight and lowering its altitude.

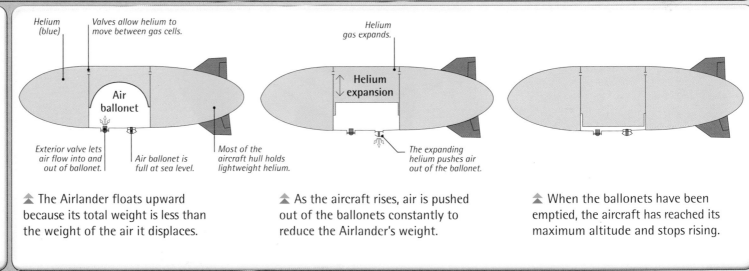

Helium (blue)

Valves allow helium to move between gas cells.

Air ballonet

Exterior valve lets air flow into and out of ballonet.

Air ballonet is full at sea level.

Most of the aircraft hull holds lightweight helium.

Helium gas expands.

Helium expansion

The expanding helium pushes air out of the ballonet.

⬆ The Airlander floats upward because its total weight is less than the weight of the air it displaces.

⬆ As the aircraft rises, air is pushed out of the ballonets constantly to reduce the Airlander's weight.

⬆ When the ballonets have been emptied, the aircraft has reached its maximum altitude and stops rising.

Winglets improve the efficiency of the wing.

◀ Flying free

Rossy makes flying his jet-powered wing look easy as he speeds through the sky over Dubai, United Arab Emirates. When fully loaded with fuel, his aircraft weighs just 121 lb (55 kg).

A helmet-mounted camera records a pilot's-eye view of the flight.

Two jet engines nestle under each side of the wing.

© Jetman Dubai

JET WING

▶▶ Swiss pilot Yves Rossy loves flying. In fact, he loves flying so much that he doesn't always bother with a plane. Instead, he transforms himself into a jet aircraft by strapping a wing and four jet engines to his back. He has flown over the Alps in Europe and Mount Fuji in Japan, and across the English Channel. Rossy has even flown in formation with the Airbus A380, the world's largest passenger airliner.

⌄ HOW IT WORKS

▶▶ The pilot wears a heat resistant flight suit similar to a firefighter's gear to protect him from the hot engines and jet exhaust. Fuel stored inside the wing flows to the engines. The engines burn the fuel and generate thrust. The pilot controls the engines with a handheld throttle.

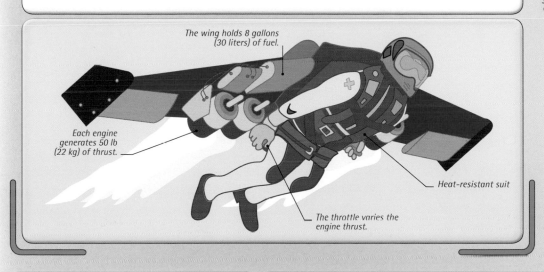

The wing holds 8 gallons (30 liters) of fuel.

Each engine generates 50 lb (22 kg) of thrust.

Heat-resistant suit

The throttle varies the engine thrust.

⌄ Flying high

▶▶ The jet-powered wing has to be launched in the air, so Rossy takes off in a plane, helicopter, or hot-air balloon—but his 6½-ft (2-m) wingspan means he has to hold on to the side, because he can't get into the craft. He starts his four jet engines and jumps from the aircraft, often launching himself with a spectacular backflip. He then fires up the engines and streaks away.

A backflip launch

◀◀ With about 80 percent throttle, Rossy flies at around 110 mph (180 kph). He adjusts how fast he's going with a small control on his right hand, and maneuvers by twisting his body or moving his hands. There are two instruments mounted on his chest: an altimeter that shows his altitude, and a timer that tells him how much fuel is left.

Jetman in mid-flight

▶▶ After almost 10 minutes, with most of his fuel gone, Rossy throttles down the engines and turns them off. He then pulls a handle to open his parachute. With the extra weight of the wing on his back, landing can be tricky. He only tries to land standing up when there is almost no wind. Usually, he has to land parallel to the ground, which can lead to scratches and scrapes.

Descending by parachute

ON THE ROAD

Since the invention of the wheel about 5,500 years ago, inventors and engineers have been searching for better, safer, and easier ways of getting around. From electric bikes and aquatic cars to slick shoes and shape-shifting cars, developers are still coming up with new and exciting ideas.

▲ EO2 car

Small cars have an advantage when it comes to parking. Few are smaller than the EO2. It's only 8½ ft (2.6 m) long, and it can make itself even smaller. The body tips up at the back, and the rear wheels tuck under the body. In addition, all four wheels can swivel 90 degrees, enabling the car to move sideways into tiny parking spaces.

▼ Copenhagen Wheel

The Copenhagen Wheel is designed to make it easier to pedal a bike, by increasing the power supplied to the wheels. The red wheel hub contains an electric motor and battery. The motor activates when the cyclist pedals, and an app lets you change the level of assistance.

⬆ WaterCar

Deep water defeats most cars, but the WaterCar Panther keeps going. The Panther is an amphibious car, equally happy on land or in water. In water, the driver pulls a lever to activate a waterjet at the back of the car, and pushes a button to raise the wheels. The waterjet propels the car. The Panther is fast enough to tow a wakeboarder or waterskier.

◀◀ Nike FlyEase

Shoes are surely the most basic type of transportation invention, but some disabilities make it difficult to tie laces. When 16-year-old American Matthew Walzer, who suffers from cerebral palsy, asked Nike to make a shoe he could put on by himself, they developed FlyEase. Instead of laces, these sneakers' wraparound zipper can be opened and closed with one hand.

▶▶ See-through truck

Drivers often find it difficult to get past a big truck safely because it blocks the view of the road ahead. One possible solution is to put a camera on the truck's hood that sends images to a screen on the truck's back. Drivers behind the truck can then see what's ahead of it, and decide when is safe to try to pass.

▼ A cavernous cargo hold

The Beluga has one of the biggest cargo holds of any civil or military aircraft in service today. It was built by converting a standard Airbus A300-600 airliner. The top of the fuselage was cut off and a new, bigger fuselage was fitted, giving it a beluga whale shape.

The front of the cargo hold opens up for loading and unloading.

A Beluga before landing

A larger-than-normal tail fin was fitted to the plane along with small stabilizer fins because the large fuselage changed the airflow around the plane.

Cargo slides from a loading platform into the plane's gaping cargo hold.

BELUGA AIRBUS

NASA's supersonic "Green Machine" concept airplane

▶▶ The Airbus A300-600ST (known as the "Beluga") cargo aircraft has been in operation since 1996. This strange-looking super-transporter was developed to carry large parts of aircraft between Airbus-manufacturing and assembly plants in Europe. Airbus maintains a fleet of five Belugas.

Supersonic aircraft

The future for commerical aircraft looks to be supersonic flight. In order for the noise levels of such flights to be bearable, concept airplanes have long, tapered bodies and V-shaped wings.

⌄ VITAL STATISTICS

▶▶ The Airbus Beluga retains the same basic dimensions as the A300-600 airliner it was developed from. It has a wingspan of 147 ft (44.8 m) and an overall length of 184 ft (56.2 m). The maximum fuselage diameter is 23 ft (7.1 m). The Beluga can carry cargo weighing up to almost 52 tons (47 metric tons) and as big as the airplane's wings. It has carried satellites, helicopters, and even large works of art.

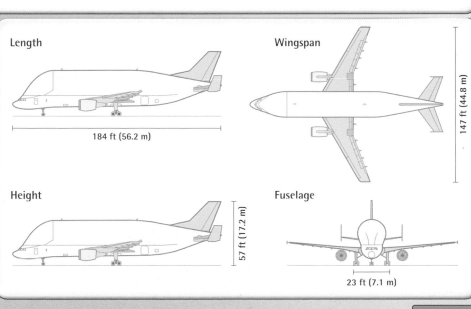

Length
184 ft (56.2 m)

Wingspan
147 ft (44.8 m)

Height
57 ft (17.2 m)

Fuselage
23 ft (7.1 m)

Beluga

The Airbus Beluga was named after the beluga whale. Belugas are not very big compared to other whales. They are only about 20 ft (6 m) long. It was the plane's shape that led to it being named Beluga.

The whale that inspired the name

Ship Intelligence

One potential future vessel, called Ship Intelligence, has been proposed by UK manufacturer Rolls-Royce. Ship Intelligence will use many technologies that the company has already developed, such as remote piloting and engines.

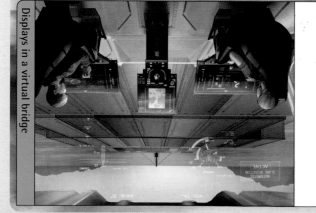

Displays in a virtual bridge

◄◄ For vessels that require a crew, the ship's bridge will have a total overhaul. The windows will become info-packed augmented reality displays, and will highlight hazards that would be difficult to spot with the naked eye. Smart workstations will recognize crew members as they enter the bridge, and adjust to their personal preferences and settings.

FUTURE SHIP

In the not-too-distant future, many of the cargo ships that crisscross oceans may be robot vessels with no crew onboard. They will be safer than crewed ships because 75 percent of all accidents at sea are caused by human error. If necessary, a crew could take control remotely from a shore-based command center. The technology and IT systems for these ships are being developed now.

Floating resorts

Cruise ships are used to transport passengers between ports of interest, but now the ships are designed as floating vacation resorts. The world's biggest cruise ship, *Oasis of the Seas*, has a park with living trees, an ice-skating rink, a zip line, and a miniature golf course to entertain its 6,000 passengers.

Oasis of the Seas

HOW IT WORKS

A European project called MUNIN (Maritime Unmanned Navigation through Intelligence in Networks) is developing the technology for operating fully autonomous vessels at sea. The equipment and the control systems are being designed so they can be fitted to existing as well as new ships.

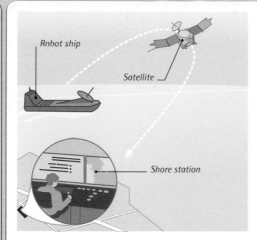

1 A ship is monitored by a human from a shore station via a satellite link.

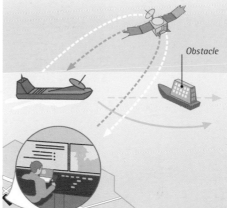

2 The ship can plot a course around an obstacle without human intervention.

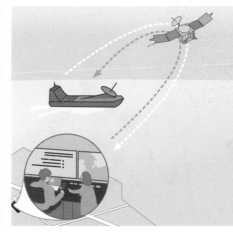

3 If required, the shore station can take control from a remote bridge.

New Horizons flew within 7,800 miles (12,500 km) of Pluto. The spacecraft was so far away from Earth that radio signals sent from the craft traveling at the speed of light took more than 4 hours to reach its researchers.

Electrical power is generated on board. The heat produced by the decay of radioactive plutonium is harnessed to produce electricity.

The crinkly gold covering on the spacecraft is a metal-coated plastic film that regulates the spacecraft's temperature.

A dish-shaped antenna 6¾ ft (2.1 m) across receives commands from Earth and sends data back.

The Solar Wind Around Pluto (SWAP) instrument measures the solar wind, the stream of particles given out by the sun.

NEW HORIZONS

▶▶ In July 2015, a grand piano–sized spacecraft took the first close-up images of the small, icy world called Pluto at the edge of the solar system. The spacecraft, New Horizons, had been flying through space for nine years to reach its target. The amazing quality of the images it beamed back meant the mission had been a total success. The spacecraft carried some of the ashes of American astonomer Clyde Tombaugh, the man who discovered Pluto in 1930.

Pluto

The images New Horizons captured of Pluto show mountains as big as the Rockies in the United States, but Pluto's mountains are made of water-ice. There are also vast plains of ice made of nitrogen, a gas on Earth, but on Pluto it's frozen solid because little of the sun's light reaches it from 3.69 billion miles (5.9 billion km) away. New Horizons photographed Pluto's five moons. The largest, Charon, is about one-third the size of our moon.

Pluto

HOW IT WORKS

▶▶ Scientists were able to reduce the amount of fuel New Horizons had to carry by using some energy from the giant planet Jupiter as the tiny spacecraft passed it. This type of maneuver is called a gravity assist, or a gravitational slingshot. New Horizons gained an extra 9,000 mph (14,500 kph) by harnessing Jupiter's gravitational pull. This boosted the craft's speed to more than 36,380 mph (53,540 kph) and cut its flight time to Pluto by five years.

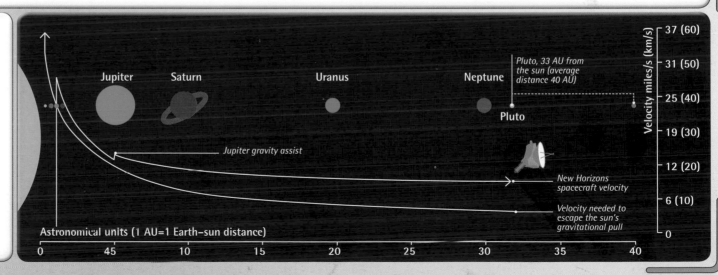

Jupiter

Saturn

Uranus

Neptune

Pluto, 33 AU from the sun (average distance 40 AU)

Pluto

Jupiter gravity assist

New Horizons spacecraft velocity

Velocity needed to escape the sun's gravitational pull

Velocity miles/s (km/s)
37 (60)
31 (50)
25 (40)
19 (30)
12 (20)
6 (10)
0

Astronomical units (1 AU=1 Earth–sun distance)
0   45   10   15   20   25   30   35   40

The Volocopter VC200 is lifted into the air by 18 electric rotors fixed to a lightweight carbon frame. More than 100 microprocessors monitor the aircraft and automatically adjust for turbulence. If the pilot lets go of the controls, the craft stays where it is.

VOLOCOPTER

If you've ever been stuck in gridlocked traffic and dreamed of flying over the top of it all, your wish may be about to come true. The Volocopter is a small aircraft designed to be easy to fly. It has seating for the pilot and one passenger. Inspired by the first toy drones that appeared in 2010, a prototype Volocopter made its first flight the following year. Unmanned and also larger passenger-carrying models are on the drawing board, meaning zipping past traffic may not be so far away.

Using the Volocopter

Volocopters could have many uses besides avoiding traffic. With a top speed of 60 mph (100 kph) and an altitude of up to 6,500 ft (2,000 m), they could be used for search and rescue, crop spraying, sports, and as an instrument platform for scientists, surveyors, and filmmakers.

Volocopter VC200

HOW IT WORKS

For takeoff, all of the Volocopter's rotors spin at the same speed, blowing air straight downward. The downward force of the rotor blades creates a reaction force according to Newton's Third Law of Motion. The reaction force is lift. This lift raises the craft up.

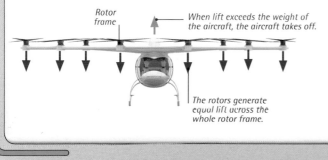

Rotor frame

When lift exceeds the weight of the aircraft, the aircraft takes off.

The rotors generate equal lift across the whole rotor frame.

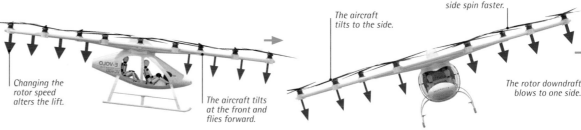

Changing the rotor speed alters the lift.

The aircraft tilts at the front and flies forward.

To fly forward, the rotors at the back spin faster than those at the front, which generates more lift at the back. The aircraft tilts forward, directing some of the downdraft from the rotors backward, which propels the aircraft forward.

The rotors on one side spin faster.

The aircraft tilts to the side.

The rotor downdraft blows to one side.

When turning to one side, the rotors on the side opposite to the turn spin faster than the rotors on the turning side, tilting the aircraft so that it is propelled sideways.

CONSTRUCT

3

All over the world, engineers and construction workers are busy turning architects' designs into breathtaking structures of steel, concrete, glass, and even ice. Skyscrapers soar higher, bridges reach farther, man-made islands appear in the ocean—and, out of sight, far beneath our feet, massive machines bore through the ground, tunneling out new road and rail networks.

How it was made

▶▶ The Burj Khalifa's foundations reach down more than 164 ft (50 m) into the ground. The basic structure used more than 11,653,840 ft³ (330,000 m³) of reinforced concrete. A staggering 37,000 tons (33,563 metric tons) of steel bars were used to build the tower.

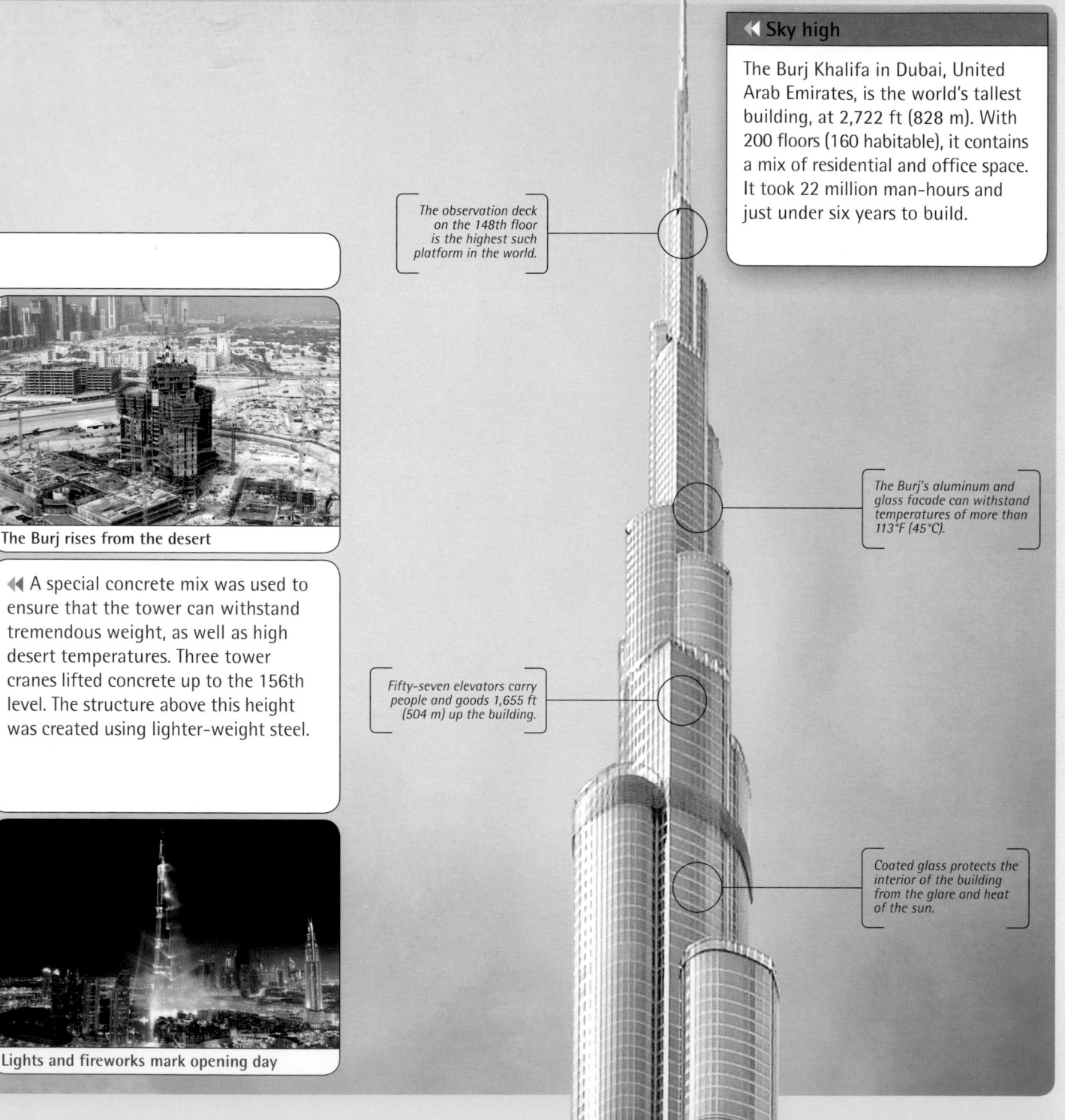

The Burj rises from the desert

◀◀ A special concrete mix was used to ensure that the tower can withstand tremendous weight, as well as high desert temperatures. Three tower cranes lifted concrete up to the 156th level. The structure above this height was created using lighter-weight steel.

Steel bars form the tower's framework

▶▶ A marvel of cutting-edge design and technology, the Burj was officially opened in January 2010. This eagerly anticipated event included a spectacular display featuring light and sound effects, as well as 10,000 fireworks. The megastructure hosts fireworks displays every New Year's Eve.

Lights and fireworks mark opening day

◀◀ Sky high

The Burj Khalifa in Dubai, United Arab Emirates, is the world's tallest building, at 2,722 ft (828 m). With 200 floors (160 habitable), it contains a mix of residential and office space. It took 22 million man-hours and just under six years to build.

The observation deck on the 148th floor is the highest such platform in the world.

The Burj's aluminum and glass facade can withstand temperatures of more than 113°F (45°C).

Fifty-seven elevators carry people and goods 1,655 ft (504 m) up the building.

Coated glass protects the interior of the building from the glare and heat of the sun.

SKYSCRAPER

▶▶ With population levels always rising, creating more places for people to live and work in often means building upward. Skyscrapers make the most of limited city space by providing thousands of homes and offices high above ground level. The first skyscrapers appeared in Chicago, Illinois, in the late 19th century. Today, they are a feature of modern cities.

The Burj's design is inspired by the patterns and styles of Islamic architecture.

The weight of the concrete used in the building equals that of 100,000 elephants.

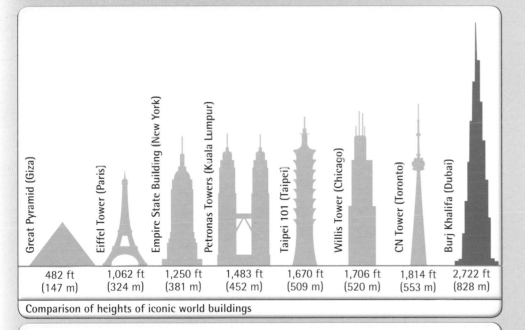

Great Pyramid (Giza)	Eiffel Tower (Paris)	Empire State Building (New York)	Petronas Towers (Kuala Lumpur)	Taipei 101 (Taipei)	Willis Tower (Chicago)	CN Tower (Toronto)	Burj Khalifa (Dubai)
482 ft (147 m)	1,062 ft (324 m)	1,250 ft (381 m)	1,483 ft (452 m)	1,670 ft (509 m)	1,706 ft (520 m)	1,814 ft (553 m)	2,722 ft (828 m)

Comparison of heights of iconic world buildings

▲ The Burj Khalifa is twice the height of the Empire State Building in New York. On a clear day, the tip of its antenna can be seen from nearly 60 miles (100 km) away. As a result of its height, it holds other records, too—such as the world's highest restaurant, observation deck, elevator system, and nightclub.

A transparent section of the walkway floor lets visitors watch sharks and other fish swimming below their feet.

The tunnel is 6³/₄ ft (2.1 m) high and 9³/₄ ft (3 m) wide, and is made of acrylic 4³/₄ in (12 cm) thick.

Sharks up to 13 ft (4 m) long swim around visitors in the tunnel.

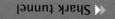

◀ Shark tunnel

In the Ocean exhibit, visitors can walk through a 52-ft (16-m) long transparent tunnel with sharks swimming around them. It's the sort of close encounter with ocean predators that is normally only experienced by intrepid divers.

BLUE PLANET

▶▶ Opened in 2013, the ultramodern Blue Planet in Copenhagen is Denmark's national aquarium. The extraordinary spiral building houses 20,000 creatures in 1.85 million gallons (7 million liters) of water. Its 53 tanks replicate the conditions in various watery habitats across the world.

Key features

▶▶ The aquarium's biggest tank, the Ocean, contains 1.1 million gallons (4 million liters) of seawater. Visitors can see sharks, rays, groupers, and other creatures through a vast 26 x 52 ft (16 x 8 m) window that is 18 in (45 cm) thick to hold the water back.

A window on the Ocean

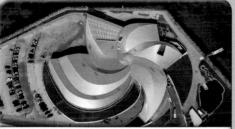

The Blue Planet from above

◀◀ The building's shape was inspired by the swirling water currents of a whirlpool. It also resembles the spiral shape of some seashells. The building is covered with thousands of diamond-shaped aluminum shingles that look like shimmering, silver fish scales.

The aquarium looks like a silver wave emerging from water at ground level

HOW IT WORKS

≫ The spiral arms that fan out from the middle of the building house five themed sections of the aquarium. The unusual spiral design means that there is no fixed route through the building, allowing visitors to explore in random and individual ways, which also reduces lines across the aquarium.

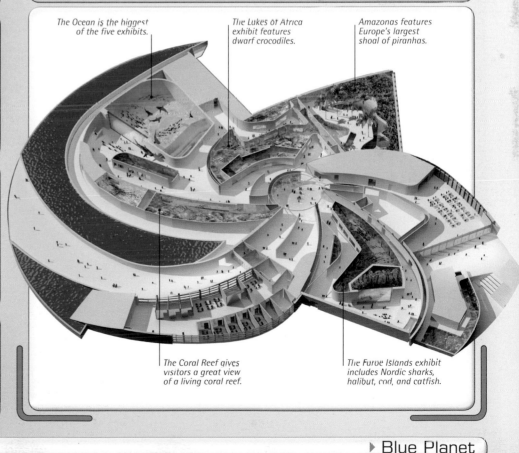

The Ocean is the biggest of the five exhibits.

The Lakes of Africa exhibit features dwarf crocodiles.

Amazonas features Europe's largest shoal of piranhas.

The Coral Reef gives visitors a great view of a living coral reef.

The Faroe Islands exhibit includes Nordic sharks, halibut, cod, and catfish.

The Icehotel has about 50 rooms, which are built to different designs each year. Most guests stay for one night. The temperature throughout the hotel is a chilly 18°F to 23°F (−5°C to −8°C), so very warm clothes are a must.

The bedrooms and public areas of the hotel are decorated with ice sculptures.

Guests sleeping on the Icehotel's ice-block beds keep warm with reindeer skins and sleeping bags.

ICEHOTEL

▶▶ One of the coolest places on Earth is the Icehotel in Jukkasjärvi, Sweden, 124 miles (200 km) north of the Arctic Circle. The entire building is made of snow and ice, and lasts over the freezing winter months only. It is redesigned and rebuilt each year using blocks of ice from the nearby River Torne and thousands of tons of snow.

⌄ HOW IT WORKS

Snow and ice are good heat insulators. People have used snow houses, called igloos, for thousands of years. Inside an igloo, air is warmed by heat rising from a fire or from people's bodies. The thick snow blocks that make the walls of an igloo trap the air, preventing the warmth from escaping too quickly.

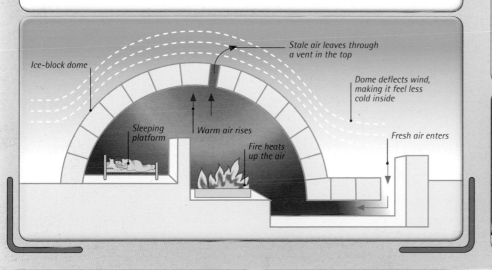

Ice-block dome
Stale air leaves through a vent in the top
Dome deflects wind, making it feel less cold inside
Sleeping platform
Warm air rises
Fresh air enters
Fire heats up the air

⌄ Building the Icehotel

▶▶ Construction begins in November, when ice blocks are placed over a metal structure. Machines are used to blow a slushy mixture of snow and ice, called snice, over them. Snice is denser than snow, provides better insulation, and doesn't melt as quickly.

Frames form the hotel's shape

Basic structure of the Icehotel

◀◀ Natural snow is packed over the snice and left to freeze for a couple of days. Compressed by its own weight, the grains of snow and ice form a strong, self-supporting structure. Next, the metal frames are removed, and the basic structure of the Icehotel stands on its own.

▶▶ More walls are built from blocks of ice that were cut from the river several months earlier and stored in a warehouse at 20°F (-7°C). About 3,000 blocks are used, each up to 3 ft (1 m) thick. Water sprayed on the blocks freezes them solid, acting in a similar way to mortar in a brick wall.

Blocks are cut with chainsaws

A peacock sculpture in the Icehotel

◀◀ Craftsmen create the hotel's interior. Builders carve blocks of ice into furniture such as beds, tables, and chairs. Artists sculpt to make wonderful likenesses of horses, bears, birds, and other animals. Even the tumblers the guests drink from are made of ice.

▲ Tent of the Khan

The Khan Shatyr Entertainment Center is the world's biggest tent. Its name means "tent of the khan." The massive structure stands 492 ft (150 m) high and covers an area of more than 1 million ft² (100,000 m²) in the city of Astana.

KHAN SHATYR

▶▶ In 2010, a dramatic new building opened to the public in Astana, the capital of Kazakhstan. Its designers had been tasked with creating a giant building with minimum internal support, so they chose a conical tent with a roof made of air-filled plastic pillows. The plastic—ethylene tetrafluoroethylene (ETFE)—is strong, lightweight, and translucent, and it hangs from a series of cables that gather at a central spire.

National Space Center Rocket Tower

⌄ HOW IT WORKS

≫ Astana's temperature can plummet to –40°F (–40°C) in winter and soar to more than 95°F (35°C) in summer, so providing a comfortable temperature all year round is a big challenge. During summer, Khan Shatyr's design makes use of the stack effect, where warm air escapes from the top, which sucks in cold air at the base. In winter, fans blow warm air along the inside of the tent to stop ice from forming.

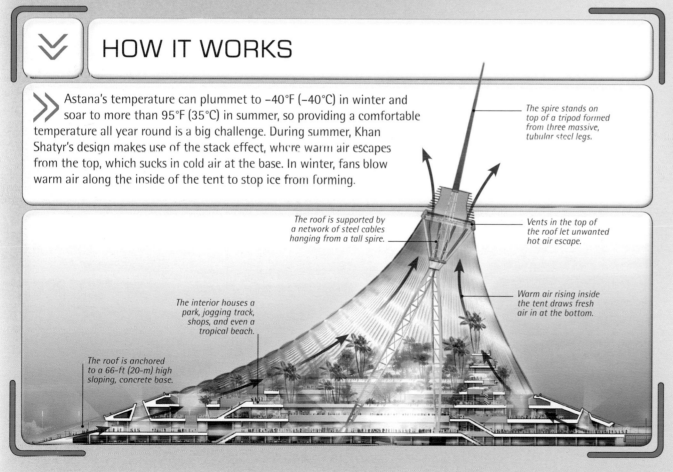

The spire stands on top of a tripod formed from three massive, tubular steel legs.

The roof is supported by a network of steel cables hanging from a tall spire.

Vents in the top of the roof let unwanted hot air escape.

The interior houses a park, jogging track, shops, and even a tropical beach.

Warm air rising inside the tent draws fresh air in at the bottom.

The roof is anchored to a 66-ft (20-m) high sloping, concrete base.

Tower of pillows

The Rocket Tower at the National Space Center in Leicester, UK, is clad with ETFE—the same material as Khan Shatyr. The 138-ft (42-m) high tower was built to house the center's biggest exhibits, including its Blue Streak and Thor Able rockets. ETFE was chosen because of its light weight, translucence, and insulation properties. The plastic is in the form of air-filled pillows, each made of three sheets of ETFE welded along their edges. They can be pumped up with more air on colder days to provide better insulation.

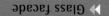

The front of the Pompidou Center is a wall of glass, which allows natural light to flood inside by day and creates a vibrant light display at night. Two-thirds of the building's wall surface is covered in a total of 118,400 ft² (11,000 m²) of glass.

POMPIDOU CENTER

▶▶ Built in the 1970s, the Centre Georges Pompidou, or Pompidou Center, was not just a new arts center for Paris, France; it was also a completely new way of designing a building. Its architects, Italian Renzo Piano and Englishman Richard Rogers, wanted to create as much open space inside the building as possible. Their solution was to turn the building inside out and put most of the internal workings of the building—the structural supports, stairways, pipework, elevators, and utilities— that are usually hidden inside, on the outside.

Colored up

▶▶ The Pompidou Center makes a feature of its pipes and girders by giving them bright colors that stand out across the city. Colors are used to highlight the functions of the components on the building. The water pipes are green, air pipes are blue, and electrical components are yellow. Red highlights lifts and stairways.

The colourful Pompidou Center

Water pipes in Berlin

◀◀ These pink pipes in Berlin, Germany, are a mixture of public works and public art. The city is built on wetland, and large construction sites would flood if the groundwater were not pumped away through this 37-mile (60-km) long network of overhead pipes.

Inside out

▲ The building is supported by a 16,500-ton (15,000-metric-ton) box of white steel columns and girders. The floors are made of reinforced concrete.

▲ Visitors can enjoy a view over Paris from a glass walkway on the roof. At seven stories high, the 138-ft (42-m) Pompidou Center is taller than most of the city's other buildings.

▲ Most of the Center's utilities are at the rear of the building. They include water pipes, air pipes, electrical components, elevators, and stairways.

▲ The front of the building is devoted to transporting visitors. Most travel through the Caterpillar—a set of escalators and walkways inside a tube suspended on the wall.

▲ Large vents are located on the roof and around the building's base to help keep the 1,111,966 ft² (103,305 m²) floor space inside supplied with fresh air.

AMAZING BUILDS

Humans have been building things for thousands of years, but these amazing designs show that there are always new things to learn. These amazing projects not only look cool, but their designs often solve problems that more traditional approaches are unable to fix.

◀◀ Canberra Arboretum

Australia's national tree collection in Canberra is built on 1 mile² (2.5 km²) of land that had been completely destroyed by a bushfire in 2003. In its place, 94 separate forests containing 48,000 trees have been planted on the landscaped hillside. They contain the rarest trees and plants from 100 different countries.

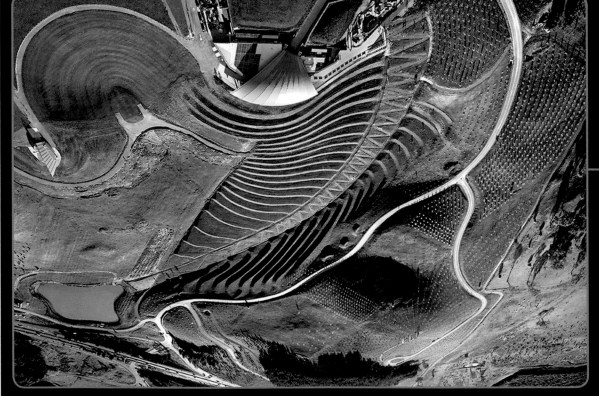

◀◀ Rolling Bridge

The Rolling Bridge crosses a canal mooring in London, UK. When boats need to pass, it simply rolls up. The bridge's deck is made of eight sections. Pistons inside the bridge's guard wall push hinged sections of the handrails up, which pull the deck into the air. Up and over it goes until the sections form a neat octagon on the far bank.

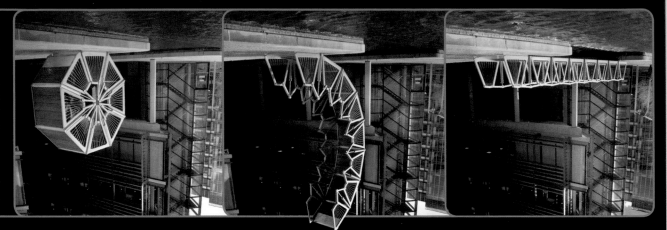

▶▶ Floating school

Makoko in Nigeria is a town built on water, with houses constructed on stilts. A new three-story school built on a raft shows a new way of building in Makoko. It floats on air-filled plastic drums and is powered by solar panels on the roof. There is a breezy terrace at the top, an enclosed classroom, and a play area on the lower level.

▼ Rotating house

Sharifi-ha House in Tehran, Iran, changes shape to suit the weather. On cold days, rotating rooms turn so their long sides form the front wall, and inside, the rooms face a covered hallway. In summer, the rooms turn outward to let the sunshine in. As they turn, the rooms create large spaces for open-air balconies protected by glass barriers.

◀◀ Telok Blangah

The rugged parklands of Singapore can be enjoyed on foot via a 3-mile (5-km) elevated walkway over steep ravines and through forests. The highlight is the Henderson Waves, a 866-ft (264-m) bridge connecting two hilltop parks. The hardwood wave along one side creates shade for walkers, but also drops beneath the deck to offer views of the city.

▶ Amazing builds

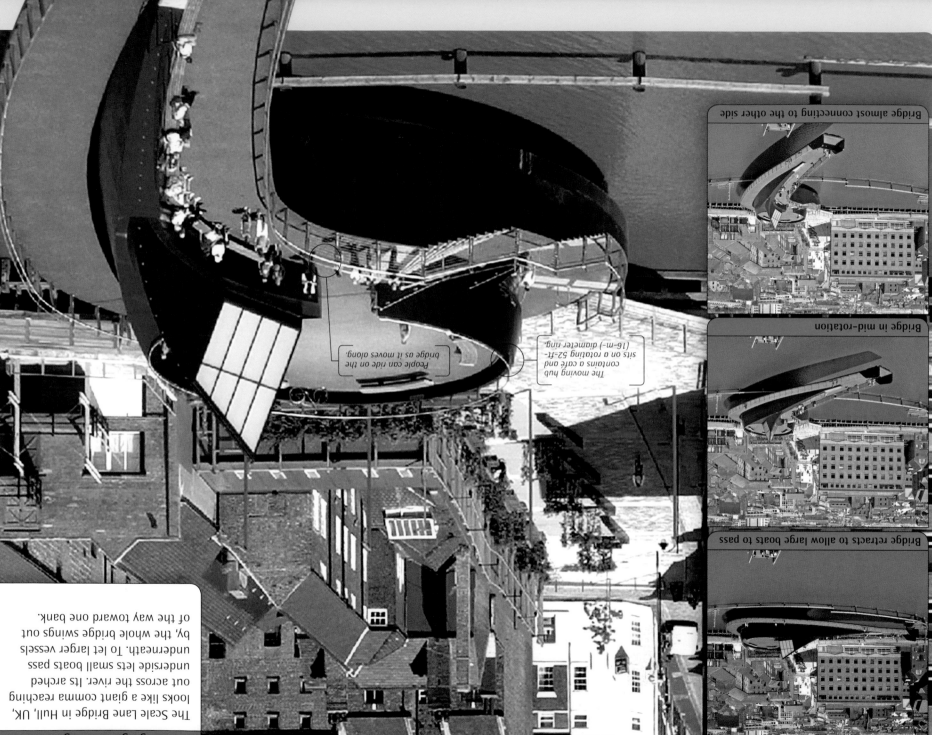

▲ Swinging footbridge

The Scale Lane Bridge in Hull, UK, looks like a giant comma reaching out across the river. Its arched underside lets small boats pass underneath. To let larger vessels by, the whole bridge swings out of the way toward one bank.

People can ride on the bridge as it moves along.

The moving hub contains a café and sits on a rotating 52-ft- (16-m-) diameter ring.

Bridge retracts to allow large boats to pass

Bridge in mid-rotation

Bridge almost connecting to the other side

CANTILEVER
BRIDGE

▶▶ Cantilever bridges are structures that project horizontally over water and are supported on one side only. The advantage of these structures is that they allow crossings over busy waterways. In recent years, designers and engineers have created some particularly innovative cantilever bridges. The 11,000-ton (1,000-metric-ton) Scale Lane Bridge, in Hull, UK, is one of them.

The 195-ft (60-m) long bridge is a cantilever counterbalanced by a heavy-circular "hub" at one end only.

HOW IT WORKS

▶▶ When a large boat is passing, lights flash and bells ring to warn people that the bridge is about to open. The bridge takes a few minutes to retract as it rotates around a 52-ft (16-m) hub, opening up a clear waterway for boats.

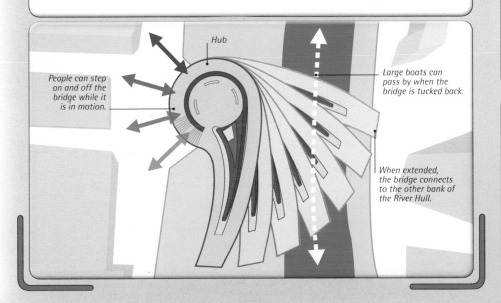

Hub

People can step on and off the bridge while it is in motion.

Large boats can pass by when the bridge is tucked back.

When extended, the bridge connects to the other bank of the River Hull.

Other amazing footbridges

▶▶ For centuries, most footbridges were simple arches or beams, but today they are often much more complex and clever structures. The Loopgraafbrug (Trench Bridge), in the Netherlands, floats on the surface of a moat around an 18th-century fort. The bridge was designed to be partially submerged because a conventional bridge above the moat would spoil the view of the site.

The Loopgraafbrug, The Netherlands

Capilano Suspension Bridge, Canada

◀◀ If you use the Capilano Suspension Bridge near Vancouver, Canada, you should definitely not have a fear of heights. Part of the bridge, the Cliff Walk, is suspended 295 ft (90 m) above the ground, on the side of a vertical cliff! Compared to other footbridges, this is one of the most thrilling walks anywhere in the world.

▶ Cantilever bridge

The Lotus Temple is composed of 27 petal-shaped structures arranged in three concentric circles of nine, forming the shape of a lotus flower. The tips of the innermost petals on top don't meet, forming a glass-covered opening that lets in sunlight.

The outermost ring of petals forms the nine entrances that encircle the building at ground level.

The petals are made of reinforced concrete that varies in thickness from 2⅜–10 in (6–25 cm).

LOTUS TEMPLE

▶▶ On the southwest side of New Delhi, India, a giant white lotus flower towers over the surrounding countryside. This strikingly beautiful structure is actually a temple, a place of worship built by the Bahá'í faith. It is India's most-visited attraction with 4.5 million people coming to see it each year.

⌄ HOW IT WORKS

⟫ Delhi can reach temperatures of 114°F (45°C). The Lotus Temple keeps the people inside cool by having openings at the base and the top of the building to draw air up through it naturally.

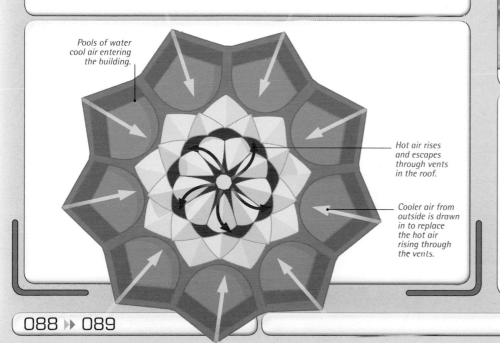

Pools of water cool air entering the building.

Hot air rises and escapes through vents in the roof.

Cooler air from outside is drawn in to replace the hot air rising through the vents.

⌄ Design and construction

▶▶ A real lotus flower floats on water, so the Lotus Temple is designed to look as if it is floating, too. It is surrounded by nine pools shaped like the floating leaves around the base of a lotus flower. The pools also have a practical purpose—they cool the air that ventilates the building.

Floating like a lotus

Meditation hall

◀◀ The Bahá'í faith, which was founded in Persia (modern-day Iran) in the 19th century, endeavors to build beautiful and distinctive places of worship and meditation. The Lotus Temple can accommodate 1,300 worshippers, and the Bahá'í faith allows for the sacred texts of other religions to be read or chanted in their temples.

▶▶ It took more than two years to convert the complex curves of the lotus shape into mathematical equations and then structural drawings. To translate the drawings into a physical structure, molds called formwork were built and filled with concrete. The concrete was then covered with white marble panels from Greece.

Interior dome

Distinct design

Despite its unusual design, the large rotunda—wider at the top than the bottom—creates a bright and open space in which to showcase artworks. The spiral path winds around the central atrium, which is where visitors enter the main gallery.

Natural light floods into the atrium from the glass dome above.

Visitors walk along a ramp that spirals up six floors.

ART GALLERY

▶▶ When the Solomon R. Guggenheim Museum of Modern Art opened in New York City in 1959, it was unlike any other place in the world. Designed by the famous American architect Frank Lloyd Wright, its unusual shape was controversial, but it quickly became a popular building that influenced other architects.

⌄ HOW IT WORKS

▶▶ The building is designed so that visitors follow a gently sloping ramp that winds around a central open space, or atrium. Radial walls divide the ramp into 70 bays where artwork is displayed. The exterior walls slope outward at the top, representing the tilt of an artist's easel.

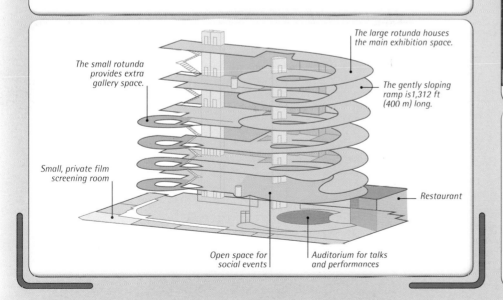

The small rotunda provides extra gallery space.

The large rotunda houses the main exhibition space.

The gently sloping ramp is 1,312 ft (400 m) long.

Small, private film screening room

Restaurant

Open space for social events

Auditorium for talks and performances

⌄ Galleries fantastic

▶▶ The iconic Guggenheim Museum includes a spiraling "drum" shape that houses the primary art gallery. The exterior of this concrete building features dramatic curves and stacked cylinders that set it apart from the surrounding buildings. The museum was renovated in 1992 (when a tower was added), and again from 2005 to 2008.

The Guggenheim, exterior view

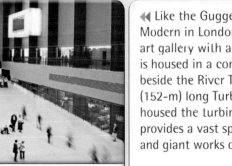
Turbine Hall, Tate Modern

◀◀ Like the Guggenheim, the Tate Modern in London, UK, is a modern art gallery with a surprising design. It is housed in a converted power station beside the River Thames. Its 500-ft (152-m) long Turbine Hall, which once housed the turbines and generators, provides a vast space for performances and giant works of art.

▶▶ One of the strangest art galleries is Art on Track. It's the world's largest mobile art gallery. The art is displayed in a passenger train in Chicago. For one day every year, each car of the train is given over to a different artist, or group of artists. The train then circles the Chicago Loop, inviting passengers to hop aboard and enjoy the art.

Art display in Art on Track

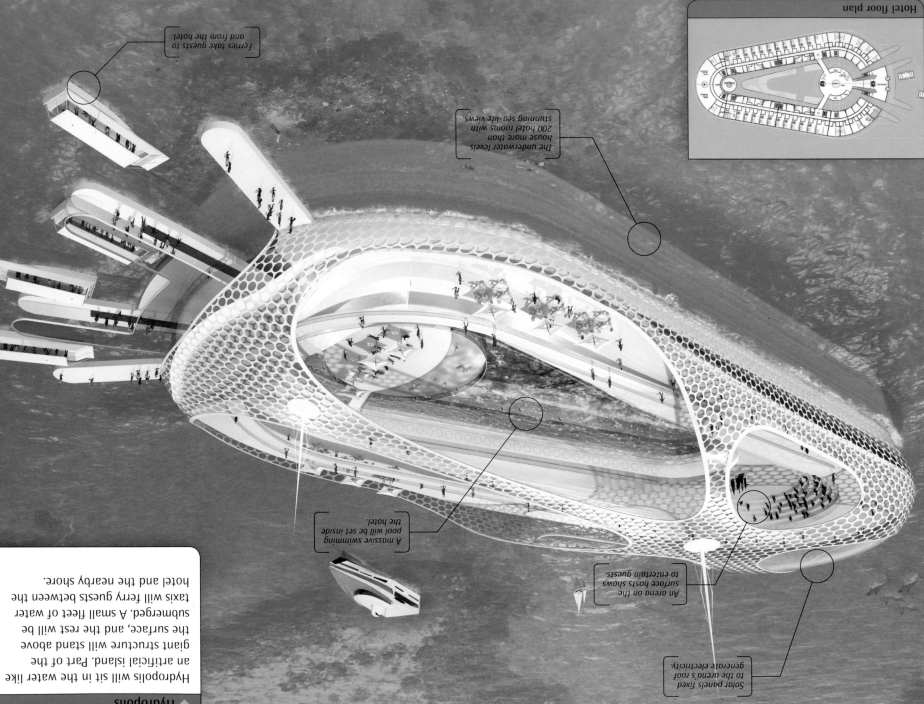

 Hydropolis

Hydropolis will sit in the water like an artificial island. Part of the giant structure will stand above the surface, and the rest will be submerged. A small fleet of water taxis will ferry guests between the hotel and the nearby shore.

Ferries take guests to and from the hotel.

The underwater levels house more than 200 hotel rooms with stunning sea-life views.

Hotel floor plan

A massive swimming pool will be set inside the hotel.

An arena on the surface hosts shows to entertain guests.

Solar panels fixed to the arena's roof generate electricity.

FLOATING
HOTEL

▶▶ Until recently, the idea of people living in the ocean was something for science-fiction stories and movies alone. All this may be about to change, however, for there are plans to build the world's first luxury hotel actually in the water. It's called Hydropolis, meaning "water city," and its vast structure, with more than 200 guest suites, will be anchored to the seabed 66 ft (20 m) below the surface. It will be one of the biggest construction projects of modern times, covering an area of 1 mile² (2.6 km²), and it is currently scheduled to be built in China.

Plus Pool

The + Pool
You can do almost anything in New York—except swim in the East River that runs through it, because the water is too dirty. The designers of the "+ Pool" (Plus Pool) aim to rectify this by building the world's first water-filtering swimming pool on the river. The floating, cross-shaped, Olympic-sized pool will be equipped with filters to clean 500,000 gallons (1.9 million liters) of river water every day of bacteria and contaminating substances. The water will then flow through the pool, enabling people to swim safely in clean river water.

HOW IT WORKS

▶▶ Hydropolis will work like a vast ship or barge tethered to the seabed by cables. Guests will arrive by ferry at one end of the hotel. From the lobby on the surface, they will descend to the three floors that are permanently underwater, giving spectacular views into the surrounding sea. Above the surface, a giant plexiglass roof will give the outdoor areas and walkways some protection from the weather. Part of the roof will be covered with solar panels to generate some of the electricity the hotel will need.

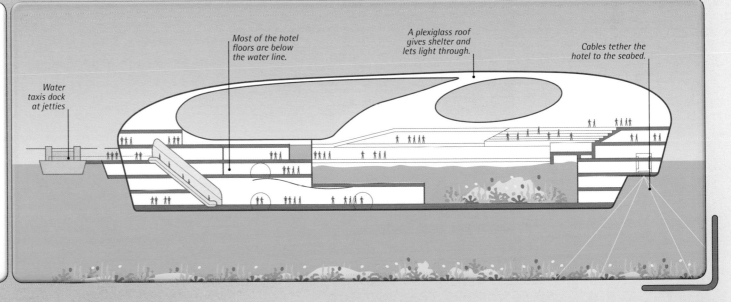

Water taxis dock at jetties

Most of the hotel floors are below the water line.

A plexiglass roof gives shelter and lets light through.

Cables tether the hotel to the seabed.

Crescent breakwater
allows the tides to
circulate water through
the artificial lagoon.

The Crescent is a 7-mile
(11-km) breakwater that
shelters the palm islands
from rough seas.

Luxurious homes

▶▶ The seafronts of Palm
Jumeirah are devoted to
luxury villas and hotel
resorts. There is room for
65,000 people to live on
the islands. A monorail
along the palm's spine
brings tourists to their
vacation destinations.

⏶ Artificial Islands

The Palm Jumeirah is the first of
several artificial island complexes
planned for Dubai. The shapes of the
artificial island systems are inspired
by nature. They must be carefully
planned to ensure the islands are
not washed away during storms.

PALM JUMEIRAH

▶▶ The Palm Jumeirah is a set of artificial islands built off the coast of Dubai, United Arab Emirates. It cost $12 billion took 40,000 workers six years to make. The islands were designed in the shape of a palm branch with 17 fronds, surrounded by a crescent, and constructed from 3.3 billion ft³ (94 million m³) of sand and rock taken from the seabed and desert inland. The Palm Jumeirah is the first of three palm-shaped islands to be constructed, which are set to transform the short desert coastline of Dubai into a city with dozens of beautiful islands and tropical beaches.

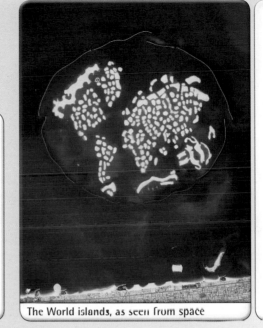

The World islands, as seen from space

See the world

All of Dubai's artificial islands are so large that they are visible from space. The latest one is The World, currently under construction along the coast from Palm Jumeirah. Its 300 islands, all for sale as private property, represent the globe's main regions. Once it is completed, the plan is to surround it with yet more islands in a development called The Universe, which will take the shape of the solar system and the Milky Way.

⌄ HOW IT WORKS

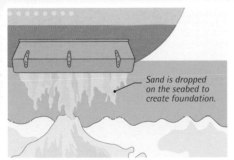

Sand is dropped on the seabed to create foundation.

▲ The original plan was to use dry desert sand for the foundations, but the sediment dredged from the seabed was found to have better results. The sand foundation is covered in a permeable plastic sheet that holds it in place.

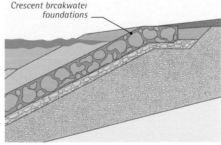

Crescent breakwater foundations

▲ The Crescent breakwater is the most robust part of the island construction. The upper layer of its foundations are covered in rocks cut from inland quarries. They create a sloping shoreline that absorbs the energy of waves.

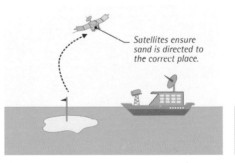

Satellites ensure sand is directed to the correct place.

▲ The location of each island was planned precisely to give the system its unique symmetry and to allow water currents to move around the islands. Satellite technology helped pinpoint suitable areas of the seabed to build on.

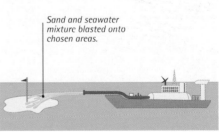

Sand and seawater mixture blasted onto chosen areas.

▲ Large pumps sprayed a mixture of sand and seawater onto the foundations to create the above-water surfaces. This layer was then shaken with vibrating probes to have the sand settle and compact, making it fit to be built on.

Mega cutter

Bertha's cutterhead, the disk that covers the entire front end of the machine, is covered in 260 cutting teeth. Their job is to break up rock and earth. The teeth wear away, so they are designed and replaced periodically.

Giant drill

BERTHA

▶▶ Whenever a new underground road or rail line is needed, a massive tunnel must be dug. To do this, we use a huge tunnel boring machine (TBM). A TBM threads its way through the ground like an enormous mechanical earthworm, grinding up the earth in front of it and spewing the debris behind. It even installs ringed concrete panels, leaving a perfectly circular tunnel. The world's largest TBM is a machine known as Bertha. It measures 328 ft (100 m) long and 57 ft (17.5 m) in diameter. It was built in Osaka, Japan, for a 2-mile (3.2-km) tunneling project in Seattle.

Constructing the tunnel

▶▶ The tunnel dug by Bertha is immediately lined with concrete blocks before the weight of the ground above distorts it. Liquid concrete called grout is then pumped behind the blocks to fill any empty spaces. As Bertha bores through the ground, it leaves a stable, waterproof, and perfectly circular tunnel behind.

Tunnel after Bertha has passed through

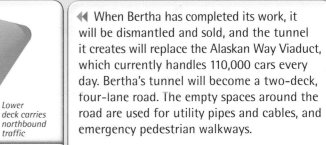

Upper deck carries southbound traffic

TUNNEL OPEN

Lower deck carries northbound traffic

Double-decker road tunnel

◀◀ When Bertha has completed its work, it will be dismantled and sold, and the tunnel it creates will replace the Alaskan Way Viaduct, which currently handles 110,000 cars every day. Bertha's tunnel will become a two-deck, four-lane road. The empty spaces around the road are used for utility pipes and cables, and emergency pedestrian walkways.

HOW IT WORKS

▶▶ Bertha is wedged into the tunnel, and then the cutterhead is pushed forward. The cutterhead rotates and its teeth grind the rock away. The broken-up rock falls into a space behind the cutterhead and a conveyor belt carries it away. Next, the jacks wedging Bertha are retracted, and the machine advances into the newly dug space. It wedges itself in place and pushes the cutterhead forward again.

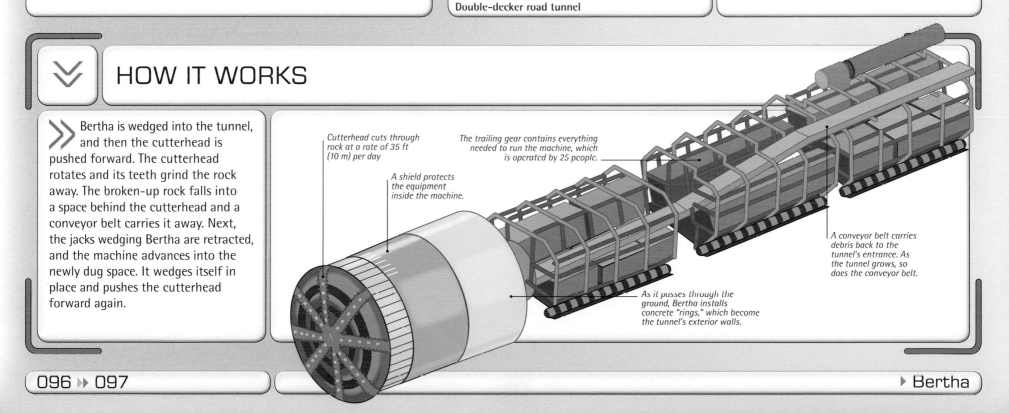

Cutterhead cuts through rock at a rate of 35 ft (10 m) per day

A shield protects the equipment inside the machine.

The trailing gear contains everything needed to run the machine, which is operated by 25 people.

A conveyor belt carries debris back to the tunnel's entrance. As the tunnel grows, so does the conveyor belt.

As it passes through the ground, Bertha installs concrete "rings," which become the tunnel's exterior walls.

MAGIC MATERIALS

One of the practical benefits of scientific research is its ability to come up with new materials for use in fields such as construction, industry, and medicine. Usually, these new materials are stronger, lighter, or more cost-effective than current materials, but sometimes they have properties that are completely new, leading to new ways of making things.

▲ Super-strong concrete

Concrete is usually reinforced internally by a steel frame. Constructing the frame is time-consuming, so scientists and engineers are testing alternative materials that might be added to concrete to strengthen it. One possibility is adding carbon nanotubes to bind the concrete together. Early tests show the nanotubes help distribute strain well, making the concrete as strong as steel-framed reinforced concrete.

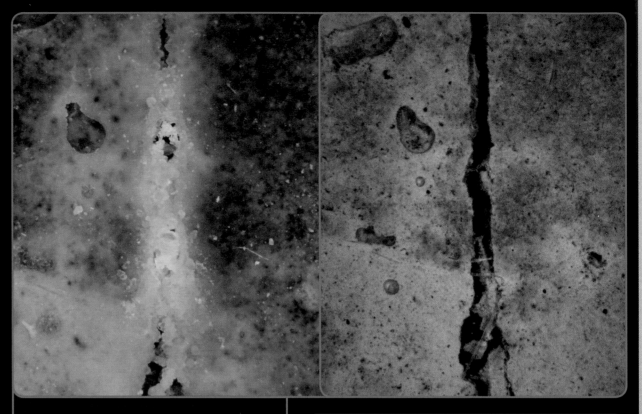

▲ Self-healing concrete

Concrete is one of the most versatile building materials, but it isn't perfect because it can be damaged and crack. The Delft University of Technology in the Netherlands has developed a solution that involves live bacteria. If the concrete cracks, water seeps in and activates the bacteria present in the concrete mix. The water causes the bacteria to produce calcite (limestone), which fills the cracks and fixes the problem.

▶▶ Self-cleaning surfaces

Walls and other surfaces attract dirt, germs, and graffiti, and the race is on to make materials that repel dirt. Scientists at the Wyss Institute at Harvard University, USA, have developed a super-efficient self-cleaning material called SLIPS (Slippery Liquid-Infused Porous Surface) that repels almost everything that touches it. SLIPS can even stop water from soaking into soft fabrics.

▼ Copying bone

Bones have a honeycomb-like inner framework that makes them strong and light. By copying this structure, researchers at Karlsruhe Institute of Technology in Germany have created a material as strong as steel and lighter than water. It is made by using a laser beam to harden light-sensitive material. A coating of alumina, a tough chemical compound, adds further strength.

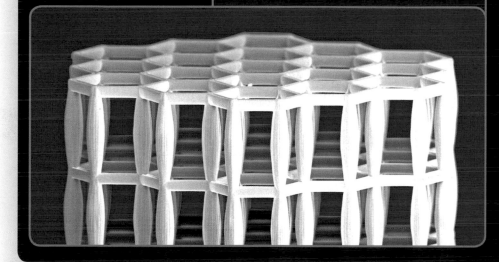

▲ Lightest-ever metal

Plane-makers are always trying to make aircraft lighter because cutting weight means saving fuel. The aerospace company Boeing has succeeded in producing a metal structure that is 99.9 percent air—lighter than polystyrene foam. The secret is its structure, which is a lattice of hollow, hairlike metal strands.

POWER

4

We need a constant supply of energy every day; the world runs on electricity from power stations to batteries. Traditionally, this electricity was produced by burning fossil fuels, but scientists are developing more environmentally sound ways of making electricity using sunlight and flowing water. Power also means strength, as some of the items in this chapter show—whether it's the tiny Raspberry Pi computer, or the massive Bagger 293 bucket-wheel excavator.

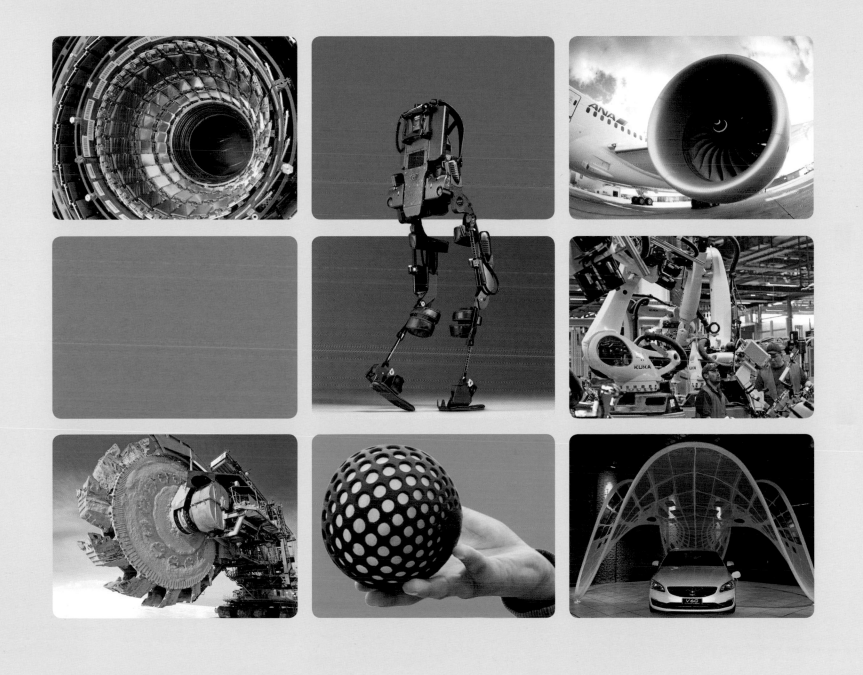

The total land area is 15½ miles² (40 km²).

Solar panels and other renewable sources will produce more energy than the factory needs.

Gigafactory

Tesla's first Gigafactory in Nevada will produce as many lithium batteries for cars as all the producers in the rest of the world put together. The factory will be powered mostly by its rooftop solar panels.

GIGAFACTORY

American car company Tesla plans to produce 500,000 affordable electric cars a year by 2020, but this would require the world's entire current global production of lithium batteries. To supply the batteries they need, Tesla is building a giant factory in Nevada called the Gigafactory. Manufacturing batteries on this scale is expected to drive production costs down by 30 percent and make their cars cheaper for consumers.

Other storage units

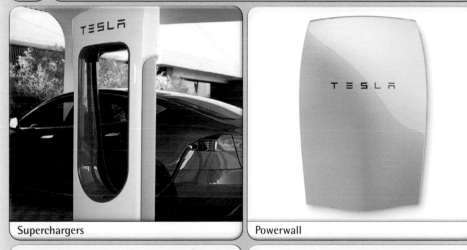

Superchargers

Powerwall

It takes several hours to charge a Tesla car battery at home, but it can be charged faster. Tesla's high-speed public superchargers can charge the battery in minutes. A 30-minute supercharge gives the car a range of 170 miles (275 km).

Tesla's Powerwall is a large battery that stores energy for powering a home. It can be charged by cheap grid electricity or energy from a renewable source such as solar panels. A high-power version called the Powerpack is made for industrial users.

HOW IT WORKS

The Gigafactory is powered by energy from the sun. It is captured by solar panels made of two different layers of impure silicon—called the P-type and N-type layers—sandwiched together. Where the layers meet, a barrier forms, through which electrons can pass in one direction only. When light strikes a panel, some electrons in the silicon become mobile. The barrier then forces them to move through wires connecting the two layers together, creating an electric current.

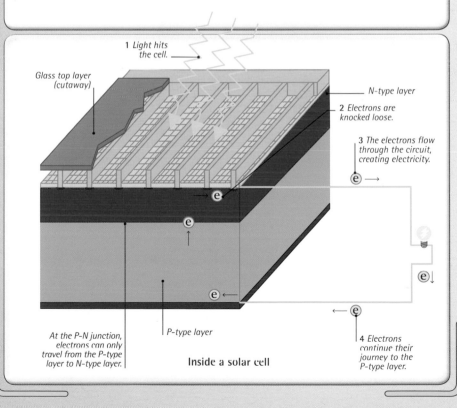

1 *Light hits the cell.*

Glass top layer (cutaway)

N-type layer

2 *Electrons are knocked loose.*

3 *The electrons flow through the circuit, creating electricity.*

At the P-N junction, electrons can only travel from the P-type layer to N-type layer.

P-type layer

4 *Electrons continue their journey to the P-type layer.*

Inside a solar cell

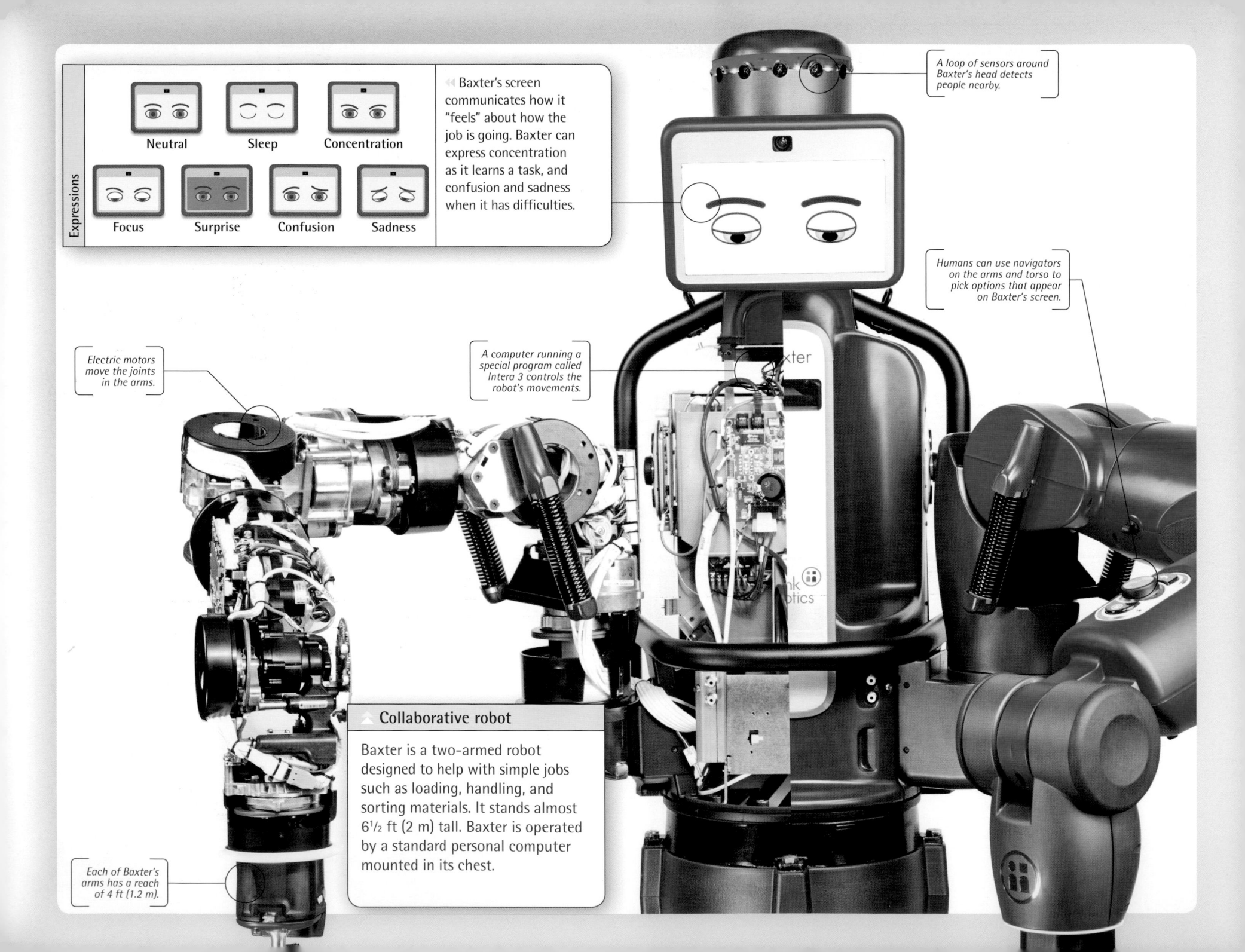

Expressions

Neutral	Sleep	Concentration
Focus	Surprise	Confusion
	Sadness	

◀◀ Baxter's screen communicates how it "feels" about how the job is going. Baxter can express concentration as it learns a task, and confusion and sadness when it has difficulties.

A loop of sensors around Baxter's head detects people nearby.

Humans can use navigators on the arms and torso to pick options that appear on Baxter's screen.

A computer running a special program called Intera 3 controls the robot's movements.

Electric motors move the joints in the arms.

Each of Baxter's arms has a reach of 4 ft (1.2 m).

▲ Collaborative robot

Baxter is a two-armed robot designed to help with simple jobs such as loading, handling, and sorting materials. It stands almost 6½ ft (2 m) tall. Baxter is operated by a standard personal computer mounted in its chest.

BAXTER

A gripper at the end of the arm can pick things up and move them around.

Baxter is a new kind of robot built to work alongside humans. Instead of being programmed like most robots, Baxter is trained by fellow workers. It can carry out simple tasks, such as sorting and loading, without posing any danger to its human coworkers.

Industrial robots

Collaborative robots, or cobots, like Baxter, are different from most industrial robots. Industrial robots are normally used for jobs that are too dangerous, dirty, or dull for humans. They are usually powerful machines used for lifting, welding, or assembling machines like cars.

Industrial robots at work in a factory

Super senses

Baxter has a camera in each wrist to give a close-up view of the objects it picks up and handles. The arms can be fitted with a parallel-jaw gripper for general use or a vacuum cup gripper for picking up flat objects.

Gripper with camera

Motorized joint

Baxter's motorized joints are equipped with sensors that detect resistance and collisions. They enable the robot to lessen the force instantly if any of its moving parts bumps into a human, reducing the chance of causing an injury.

HOW IT WORKS

A typical job for Baxter might be picking up parts from a conveyor belt and packing them in a box. Once Baxter is shown how to do the job by a coworker, it can carry out the task without supervision. Its facial expressions show whether it is struggling or finding the task manageable.

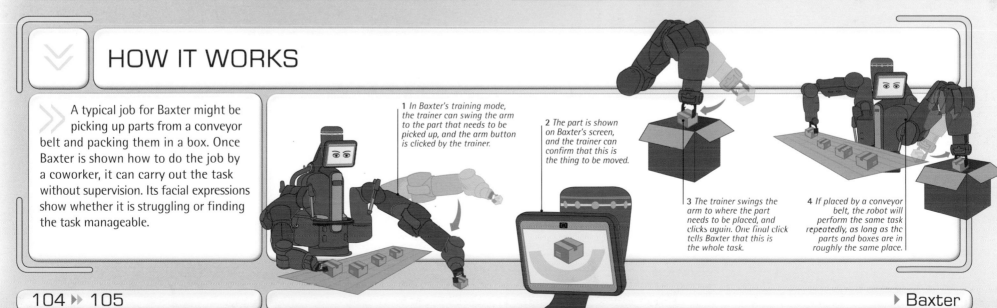

1 In Baxter's training mode, the trainer can swing the arm to the part that needs to be picked up, and the arm button is clicked by the trainer.

2 The part is shown on Baxter's screen, and the trainer can confirm that this is the thing to be moved.

3 The trainer swings the arm to where the part needs to be placed, and clicks again. One final click tells Baxter that this is the whole task.

4 If placed by a conveyor belt, the robot will perform the same task repeatedly, as long as the parts and boxes are in roughly the same place.

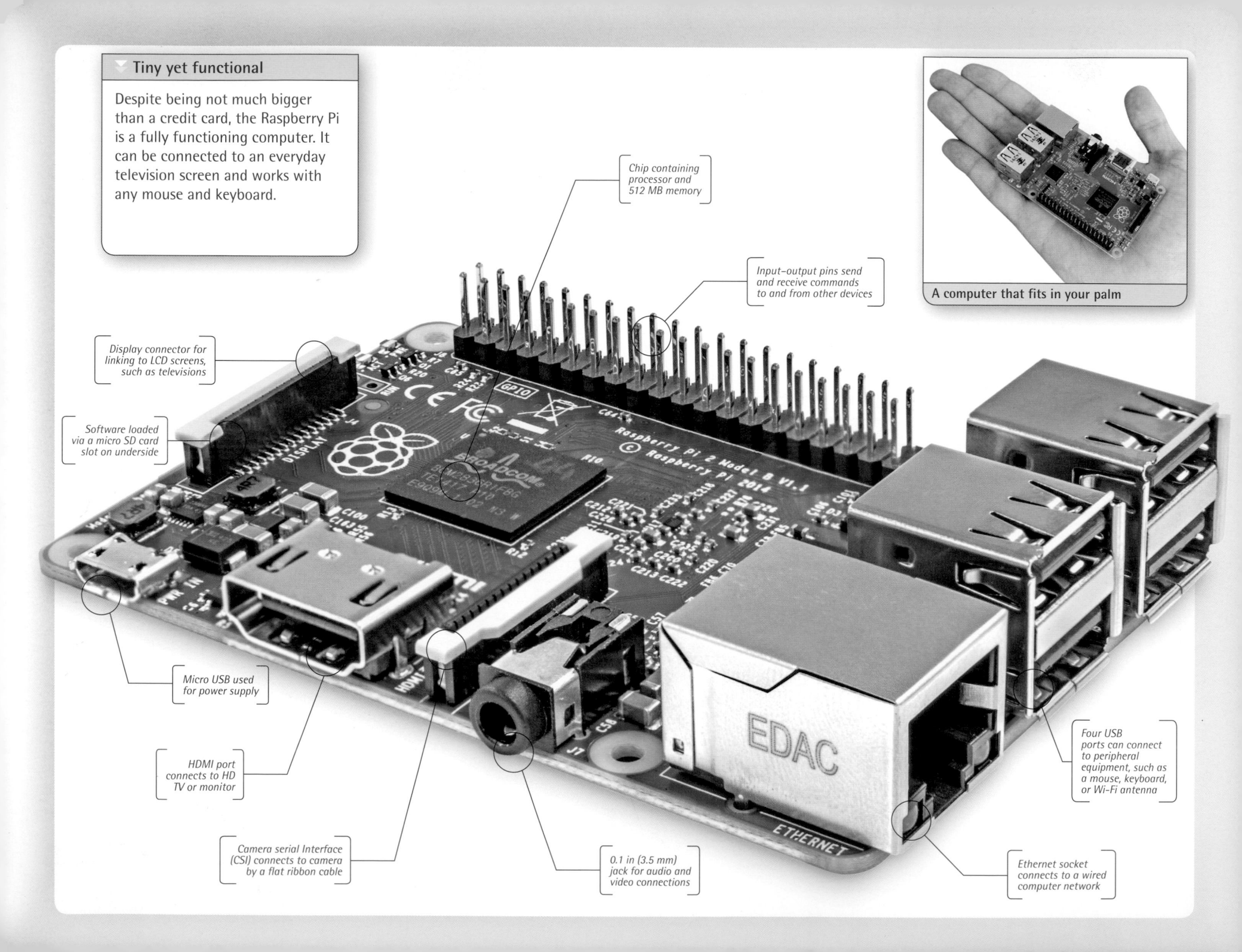

Chip containing processor and 512 MB memory

Input–output pins send and receive commands to and from other devices

A computer that fits in your palm

Display connector for linking to LCD screens, such as televisions

Software loaded via a micro SD card slot on underside

Micro USB used for power supply

HDMI port connects to HD TV or monitor

Camera serial Interface (CSI) connects to camera by a flat ribbon cable

0.1 in (3.5 mm) jack for audio and video connections

Four USB ports can connect to peripheral equipment, such as a mouse, keyboard, or Wi-Fi antenna

Ethernet socket connects to a wired computer network

EDAC

RASPBERRY PI

▶▶ The Raspberry Pi is as simple as a personal computer gets. Designed as a small motherboard (a circuit board that has all the basic elements of a computer), the Raspberry Pi is a fraction of the price of even a basic desktop computer. The Pi has no internal hard disk, and all software is stored on a Secure Digital (SD) card created especially to control the computer. It can play videos, connect to the Internet, and run everyday applications. Also, its low cost and small size makes the Raspberry Pi ideal as a programming tool, used to create your own games and music, control homemade robots, or whatever else you can dream up.

HOW IT WORKS

As well as working like a regular computer, the Raspberry Pi is built to connect to all kinds of other devices. These are known as HATs, short for "Hardware Attached on Top," because they are sized to screw in place over the motherboard. A HAT can carry any device, from altitude detectors to thermometers. This robot car is controlled by a program running on the Raspberry Pi inside while connected to a HAT. The HAT drives the motors on each wheel and is connected to detectors that tell the robot what is around it.

HACKABALL

The Hackaball is a computer that has been designed as a fun way of introducing children to the basics of computer programming. By using an app, kids can design and program their own games for the ball—such as "pass the bomb" or "keepie-uppie"—by setting up a simple set of rules and instructions. It is tough enough to be bounced, thrown, kicked, and rolled, and is also sensitive to motion and can change color, vibrate, and make sounds. The Hackaball can be reprogrammed—meaning the instructions can be changed—to improve and alter the games available.

Hackaball is part toy, part programming device

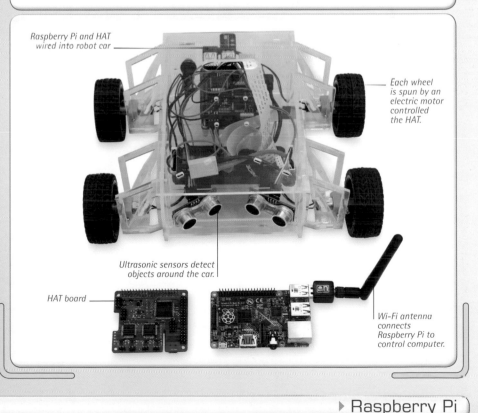

Raspberry Pi and HAT wired into robot car

Each wheel is spun by an electric motor controlled the HAT.

Ultrasonic sensors detect objects around the car.

HAT board

Wi-Fi antenna connects Raspberry Pi to control computer.

The wheel has giant buckets around its edge that tear into the ground and scoop earth up.

A wide base spreads the immense weight of the machine over a large area to keep it from sinking.

◄ Mammoth digger

This giant bucket-wheel excavator is used at a mine in Germany. Each of its buckets is as big as a family car. The biggest of these machines can dig up to 8.5 million ft³ (240,000 m³) of coal a day, or enough to fill 96 Olympic swimming pools.

BUCKET-WHEEL
EXCAVATOR

In places where coal lies close to the surface, the most efficient way to reach it is to strip away the soil and rock that lies on top of it. Machines called bucket-wheel excavators are often used for this task, and they are some of the biggest land vehicles ever built. The largest of these is the Bagger 293. From end to end it measures 738 ft (225 m) and stands 315 ft (96 m) tall. It tips the scales at a whopping 15,650 tons (14,200 metric tons), making it the world's heaviest land vehicle.

Caterpillar 8750

Other big diggers

Bucket-wheel excavators are not suitable for every digging job. There are other giant diggers for these jobs. The biggest single-bucket diggers are draglines. These machines lower a huge bucket to the ground and drag it back toward the digger, scooping up earth on the way. Smaller excavators move on tracks or wheels, but big machines like the Caterpillar 8750 walk on giant feet!

HOW IT WORKS

The excavator's bucket wheel is attached to a boom that is connected to a central platform. The position of the bucket wheel can be changed by the boom. When operated, the bucket wheel is lowered into the ground, and it slowly cuts into the earth. As the buckets rotate, the earth is deposited on to a conveyor belt that carries it along the boom and away for processing.

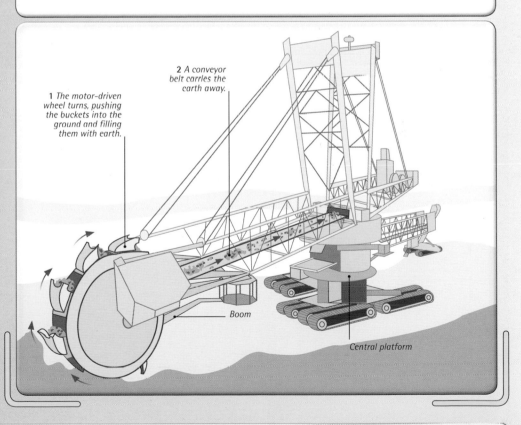

2 A conveyor belt carries the earth away.

1 The motor-driven wheel turns, pushing the buckets into the ground and filling them with earth.

Boom

Central platform

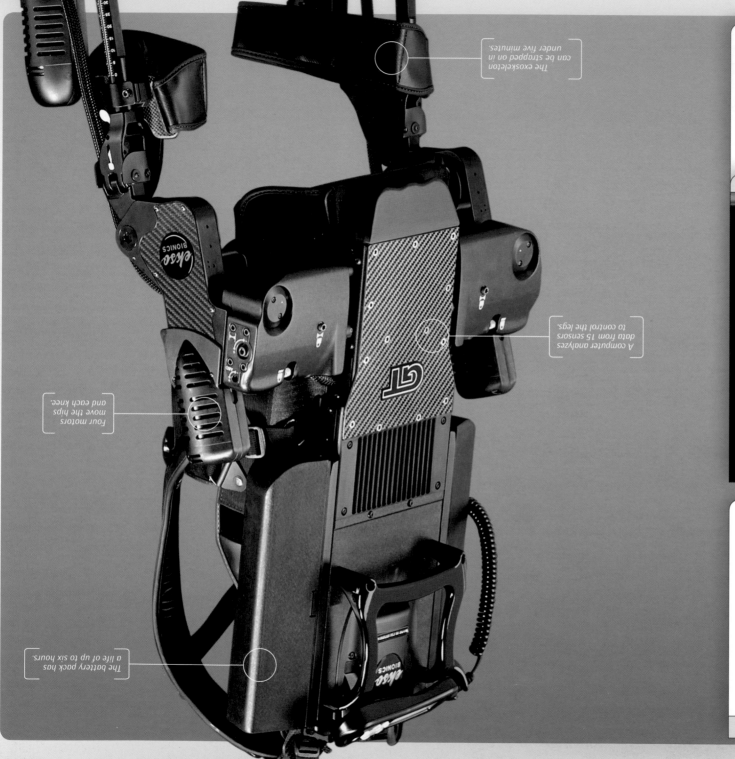

The exoskeleton can be strapped on in under five minutes.

A computer analyzes data from 15 sensors to control the legs.

Four motors move the hips and each knee.

The battery pack has a life of up to six hours.

Extra support

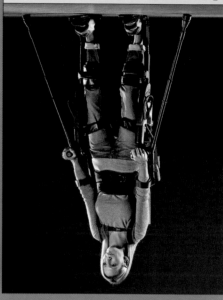

The Ekso suit can be used with a variety of additional supportive equipment to help get its wearer upright and walking. A walking frame, crutches, or a walking stick can give the extra support needed until the wearer is able to walk unaided.

Walking unassisted

The Ekso exoskeleton is a wearable robot. It straps to the waist, shoulders, and legs, together with a backpack containing the suit's computerized control system and batteries. The exoskeleton can be operated by a therapist using a remote control until the wearer gets the hang of using it. After building muscle power, the user can take control and walk unassisted.

BIONIC
SUIT

▶▶ Injuries to the spinal cord can be catastrophic. Depending on the location and severity of the injury, it can mean a lifetime in a wheelchair. Other conditions, such as a stroke, can cause weakness in the legs that makes walking difficult. American company Ekso Bionics's powered exoskeletal (external skeleton) suit is designed to help people with these problems. Originally conceived as a device to give people superhuman strength for lifting heavy loads, powered exoskeletons can also enable wheelchair-bound people to walk again.

Ironclad beetle

Exoskeletons in nature

Nature invented the exoskeleton, long before engineers thought of it. Animals such as crabs, lobsters, beetles, and spiders all have exoskeletons. The hard exterior protects the creature from predators, but it makes growth difficult. To grow, the animal must shed its exoskeleton to develop a new, bigger one.

The leg length can be adjusted to suit the wearer's body shape.

The path of each foot is adjusted 500 times a second to prevent stumbling.

An underground giant

▶▶ Looking like the inside of a high-tech washing machine, this is the Compact Muon Solenoid (CMS), a detector in the Large Hadron Collider. It is 49 ft (15 m) wide, weighs 15,400 tons (14,000 metric tons), and is housed in a cavern 328 ft (100 m) below ground.

LARGE HADRON
COLLIDER

▶▶ The Large Hadron Collider (LHC) is the largest and most complex scientific instrument ever built. It studies the science of subatomic particles by speeding them up to almost the speed of light before smashing them together, to see the even smaller bits that are flung out. The energy released in these collisions is like miniature recreations of the Big Bang.

HOW IT WORKS

▶▶ A series of accelerators boost the speed of subatomic protons until they can be injected into the LHC. Two beams of protons in side-by-side tubes circle in opposite directions. The beams cross at four places—CMS, LHC-b, ATLAS, and ALICE—where different experiments record the results of collisions between the particles.

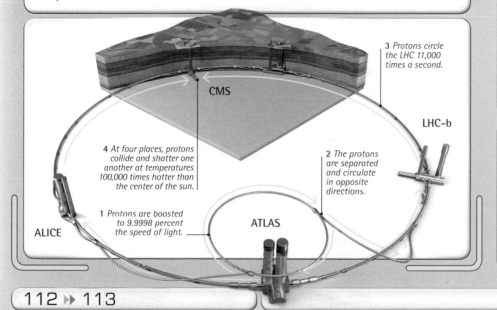

3 Protons circle the LHC 11,000 times a second.

CMS

LHC-b

4 At four places, protons collide and shatter one another at temperatures 100,000 times hotter than the center of the sun.

2 The protons are separated and circulate in opposite directions.

1 Protons are boosted to 9.9998 percent the speed of light.

ALICE

ATLAS

A rundown of the main experiments

▶▶ The Compact Muon Solenoid (CMS) is one of two general-purpose particle detectors in the LHC, the other being ATLAS. CMS was used in the successful search for the Higgs boson particle, and is crucial in dark matter studies and the search for possible extra dimensions.

CMS

▶▶ LHC-b is used to investigate why there seems to be much more matter than antimatter in the universe. Equal amounts should have been produced by the Big Bang, but matter dominates the universe today. The "b" in LHC-b stands for "beauty."

LHC-b

▶▶ ATLAS stands for A Toroidal LHC ApparatuS. It has the same goals as the CMS detector, but it uses different equipment and methods. It tracks the path, momentum, and energy of particles that fly out of proton collisions.

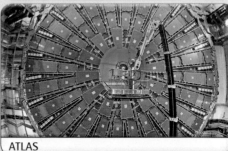

ATLAS

▶▶ A Large Ion Collider Experiment (ALICE) was built to study how tiny particles called quarks combined to form the larger subatomic particles like protons and neutrons that we see today. To find this out, ALICE smashes lead nuclei, and not protons, together.

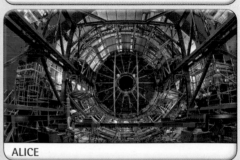

ALICE

LIGHTEN UP

Light is a very useful, and free, source of energy, and inventors are busy creating new products that use it and produce it. They use solar panels to change light into electricity, and they concentrate light with mirrors so that it generates high temperatures. They've also discovered how to make a brand-new material called graphene produce light.

◀◀ Solar pavilion

To show off the the V60, their hybrid electric/gas car, Swedish car company Volvo designed a collapsible pavilion that featured solar panels. The beautiful pavilion can fold up to fit in the trunk, meaning it can be used to charge the car wherever you go.

◀◀ GoSun

The GoSun solar stove uses nothing more than sunlight to produce temperatures high enough to cook food. Food is placed on a long, thin tray, which slides inside a glass tube. Reflectors focus sunlight on the tube and heat it up. The stove can cook a meal in 20 minutes at a temperature of up to 550°F (288°C).

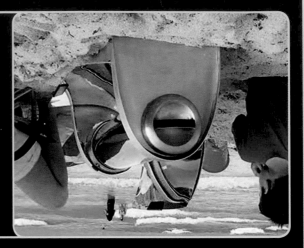

◀◀ Revolights

Being seen by other road users is important for cyclists. Revolights make bikes easy to see by lighting up light-emitting diodes (LEDs) on the wheels, white at the front and red at the back. The system detects the bike's speed and lights the LEDs only when they are at the front of the front wheel and the back of the rear wheel.

⬆ Solar-powered socket

There are lots of solar-powered batteries and chargers, but this product is the first solar-powered socket. When it is stuck to a sunlit window, a solar panel on the sticky side generates electricity and charges a built-in 1,000 mAh battery. A phone, tablet, or other device can be plugged into a socket on the other side of the unit.

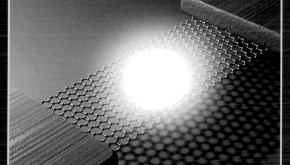

◀◀ Graphene bulb

Researchers have discovered how to make a light bulb from the new wonder material, graphene, an ultrathin honeycombed form of carbon. When an electric current flows through a strip of graphene, heat is generated. It can reach a temperature of up to 4,590°F (2,530°C) and glow brightly. In the future, this could help microchips communicate with each other by using light.

The solar panels
generate electricity
to charge a battery.

Tracking the sun

The SOFT Rocker gently rocks and
rotates as the person inside it shifts
position. By adjusting the rocker's
angle, the sitter can lounge
comfortably in the shade while
keeping the solar panels directly
facing the sun.

SOFT ROCKER

▶▶ Relaxing in a shaded lounge chair on a summer's day can recharge your batteries in more ways than one. Architects at the Massachusetts Institute of Technology (MIT) have come up with a way of using the sun to charge your gadgets while you recline in comfort. Knowing that things like awnings and umbrellas soak up solar energy, which then goes to waste, MIT students helped design a lounge chair that would make use of this free energy. The result is the SOFT Rocker, a futuristic piece of outdoor furniture that generates free electricity while you lounge.

Using free energy

▶▶ State-of-the-art thin-film solar panels on top of the SOFT Rocker charge a 6-volt, 12 amp-hour battery. This battery can charge up to three phones at the same time in about four hours and can top up many other electronic devices, too. It also stores energy taken in during the day, so it can be used at any time, even at night. The SOFT Rocker's curvy shape is designed to hold the solar panels at the right angle for maximum sun exposure on the MIT campus, but it could be adapted for any site.

Charging a smartphone

Electricity-generating plastic

◀◀ After dark, the SOFT Rocker's battery powers an electroluminescent (EL) strip inside the lounge chair. The strip is made of a semiconducting material that can be cut to any length. It lights up when an electric current from the Rocker's battery flows through it. Like a light-emitting diode (LED), the strip produces light without heat, bathing the lounge chair in a soft colored glow.

Solar windows

Most of the solar energy that reaches Earth's surface is wasted. If more solar panels were used in construction, buildings could generate electricity in the same way as the SOFT Rocker. Researchers working on ways of harnessing sunlight have developed an electricity-generating plastic panel. Just one skyscraper clad in this new material would make a vast amount of electricity.

The SOFT Rocker as night falls

▲ Air power

The big, 20-bladed fan at the front of the Trent 7000 gives this type of engine its name—turbofan. The spinning fan generates three-quarters of the engine's thrust. Only 10 percent of the air from the fan enters the engine's hot core.

JET ENGINE

With more than 50,000 in action across the globe, the Rolls-Royce company is world-famous for its jet engines. The Trent is one of its most successful engine families, powering the Airbus and Boeing airplanes. The latest model is the Trent 7000, developed for the new Airbus A330 neo twin-engine airliner. It is about 50 percent quieter and 10 percent more fuel-efficient than previous Trent engines.

Queen Elizabeth Class aircraft carrier

Marine turbines

Trent engines are not only found on airliners. A variant of the Trent, the Marine Trent, powers warships. Instead of producing a jet of gas to thrust an aircraft through the sky, the Marine Trent uses its power to turn a ship's propellers to move the ship forward. The British Royal Navy's newest aircraft carriers, the Queen Elizabeth Class, are powered by the Marine Trent. These ships, at a weight of 71,650 tons (65,000 metric tons), are the biggest surface ships ever operated by the Royal Navy.

HOW IT WORKS

The spinning fan sucks in enough air to fill a racquetball court every second. A compressor squeezes it to one-fiftieth of its volume. Burning fuel heats it to 2,900°F (1,600°C). The gas expands rapidly, jetting out of the engine through the turbine, helping propel the airplane forward.

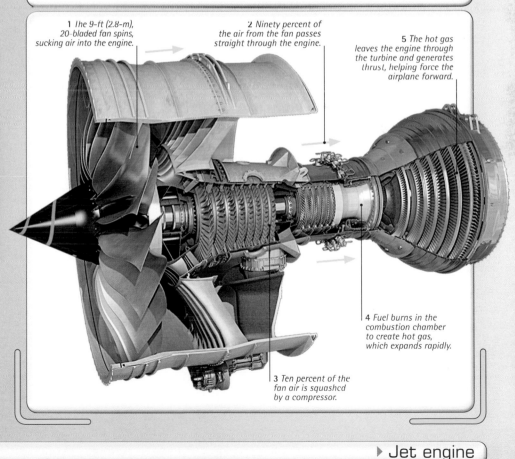

1 The 9-ft (2.8-m), 20-bladed fan spins, sucking air into the engine.

2 Ninety percent of the air from the fan passes straight through the engine.

5 The hot gas leaves the engine through the turbine and generates thrust, helping force the airplane forward.

4 Fuel burns in the combustion chamber to create hot gas, which expands rapidly.

3 Ten percent of the fan air is squashed by a compressor.

▲ **Water power in action**

China's Three Gorges Dam is nearly 1½ miles (2.3 km) long and 594 ft (181 m) high. Water from the reservoir behind the dam drives its turbines, producing 22,500 megawatts of electricity. A lift allows big ships to traverse the dam.

HYDROELECTRIC DAM

Hydroelectric dams are massive concrete structures that generate electricity by using energy extracted from moving water. The biggest in the world is the Three Gorges Dam in Hubei, China. Standing across the mighty Yangtze River, its 34 turbines can generate 20 times the energy output of a nuclear power station. There were proposals for a dam on the Yangtze to generate electricity and control flooding as long ago as 1919, but construction didn't actually begin until 1994. It was completed 14 years later, in 2008, and became fully operational in 2012.

Collecting garbage in the reservoir

Trash collection

Though the dam is seen as a modern wonder, an unavoidable downside is that it collects everything thrown into the river. More than three tons of trash is removed every day. During the rainy season, it can get so bad that people are able to walk across the garbage islands that develop.

HOW IT WORKS

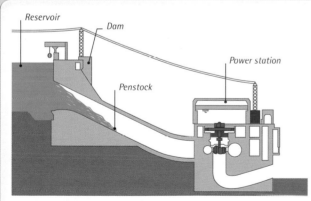

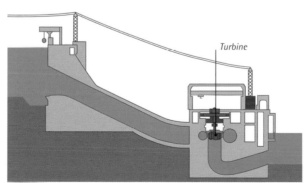

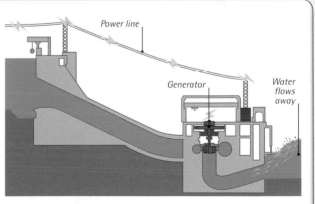

⬆ Water from the reservoir enters a huge pipe called a penstock. This guides the water downhill, gathering speed, toward the power plant's turbines.

⬆ The fast-flowing water hits the blades of a row of turbines. The water transfers some of its energy to the turbines, making them spin at high speed.

⬆ Each turbine is connected to a generator. The spinning turbine drives the generator. This produces electricity, which is carried away by power lines.

There are countless appliances of all kinds that help make our lives easier, longer, or more enjoyable. Thanks to some smart thinking, it is now possible to make drinking water out of thin air, see through bionic eyes, and even teach our pets to play electronic games. Scientists and engineers are not just looking at ways of making life on Earth better, though. They are working on the technology that will allow us one day to leave the planet to also live on our neighbor Mars.

LIVE

The wearer is able to stay in touch with other firefighters through the helmet.

A thermal image shows where the hot spots are, even if they are hidden behind thick smoke.

204
UMEÅ-SD

INFRARED CAMERA

A helpful wire-frame image of the surroundings is superimposed on what the firefighter sees.

▲ Seeing through the smoke

The C-Thru Smoke Diving Helmet aims to provide firefighters with all of the information they need to find people in burning buildings, without the need to carry extra equipment. Firefighters who primarily work inside burning buildings are called "smoke divers."

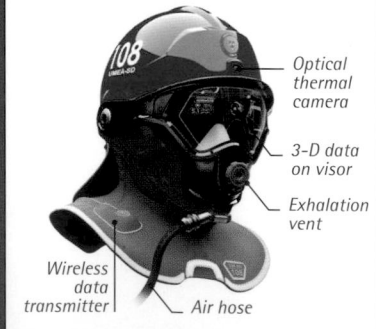

Hi-tech helmet

108
UMEÅ-SD

- Optical thermal camera
- 3-D data on visor
- Exhalation vent

Wireless data transmitter
- Air hose

Easy to wear

Firefighters usually need to be ready for action in 90 seconds after a call, so the C-Thru Helmet is designed to be put on quickly and easily, even at night in a fire engine going at full speed.

C-THRU
HELMET

▶▶ Though their name suggests they only battle flames, firefighters have another, more dangerous, foe, in the form of smoke. When dense smoke fills enclosed spaces, visibility is zero, and firefighters have to find their way around by touch and hearing. Nobody inside a burning building can survive beyond a few minutes in the choking atmosphere, including those trying to rescue people. Using a combination of incredible technologies, a concept helmet called the C-Thru has been designed to give firefighters some crucial advantages over current equipment when out trying to save people's lives.

Armored divers

Like firefighters, people who venture into other extreme environments have to wear protective clothing and life-support systems. One of the most dangerous places on Earth is at the bottom of an ocean. The pressure of the water will crush divers to death unless they are protected by an atmospheric diving suit. Resembling a suit of armor, this suit enables a diver to breathe and work at depths of 2,000 ft (600 m). At this level, pressure is 60 atmospheres, or 60 times the atmospheric pressure at the surface of the ocean.

A diver in an atmospheric diving suit

⌄ HOW IT WORKS

▶▶ The C-Thru Helmet includes image processing, communication, and audio systems. An optical thermal camera on the front of the helmet captures image data from the situation. The data is transmitted to a device held by the firefighters' team leader outside the building. This device processes the data and transmits it back to the firefighters' helmets, which project it on the visor. To improve hearing as well as vision, the helmet's audio system cancels the sound of the wearer's breathing and unimportant noise.

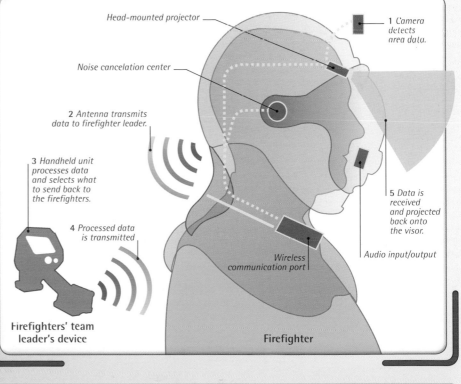

Head-mounted projector

1 Camera detects area data.

Noise cancelation center

2 Antenna transmits data to firefighter leader.

3 Handheld unit processes data and selects what to send back to the firefighters.

4 Processed data is transmitted

5 Data is received and projected back onto the visor.

Wireless communication port

Audio input/output

Firefighters' team leader's device

Firefighter

CleverPet's games include encouraging the dog to remember a sequence of lights, respond to audio commands, or touch the lights when they flash. As the dog learns, the games get faster and more difficult, with new games available to download via Wi-Fi.

The dome contains a food hopper that holds two or three cups of dry dog food.

The food tray is hidden until the dog presses the correct touch pad. Then it rotates into view with a treat for the dog to eat.

Touch screen–like interactive pads light up.

CLEVERPET

▶▶ Just like people, animals get bored when they have nothing to do. The answer for owners who have to leave their dogs alone at home could be an electronic device called CleverPet. This is a gaming console that uses lights and sound to give dogs various puzzles to solve, with tasty rewards for correct responses. Puzzles include remembering sequences of lights and responding to audio cues.

⌄ HOW IT WORKS

⟩⟩ For the light-sequence game, the machine plays a pattern of flashing lights. The dog must then touch the pads in the right order, which is registered by the pads. If the dog gets a sequence right, a mechanism called a worm gear, consisting of a threaded screw and a toothed wheel, drives around a food tray carrying a small treat. The dog takes the reward and the tray rotates out of sight again. Inside the dome, another treat drops onto the tray, ready for the next game.

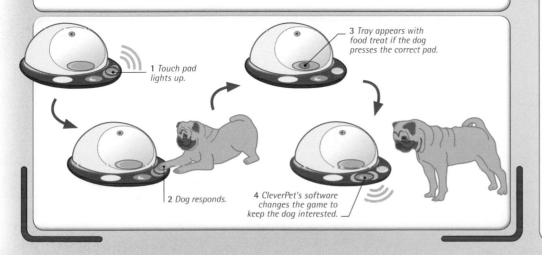

1 Touch pad lights up.

2 Dog responds.

3 Tray appears with food treat if the dog presses the correct pad.

4 CleverPet's software changes the game to keep the dog interested.

⌄ Smart gadgets for pets

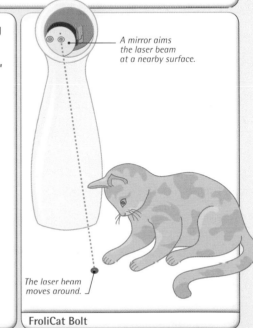

The collar comes in different sizes to suit the dog.

A GPS antenna tracks location.

WÜF collar

⬆ Pet owners can choose from a variety of smart gadgets designed especially for animals. One of these devices, called WÜF, is a sort of activity tracker for dogs. Worn like a collar, it tracks the dog using GPS and also monitors the dog's daily activities. Using an app and a smartphone, an owner can talk to a dog via a loudspeaker in the collar—and the dog's bark back can be heard, because WÜF also has a built-in microphone.

▶▶ It's not just dogs that are having all of the techie fun. Cats can get in on the act with the FroliCat Bolt, a laser toy that shines a bright moving dot on the floor for the cat to chase and pounce on. The random laser patterns are designed to stimulate a cat's natural hunting instincts. An automatic timer switches the toy off after 15 minutes of feline fun. These sorts of playthings are designed to give cats exercise and entertainment, especially if they live indoors all the time.

A mirror aims the laser beam at a nearby surface.

The laser beam moves around.

FroliCat Bolt

▶▶ The house of tomorrow

The amazing, shape-shifting D*Dynamic house rotates on special rails set into the ground. It doesn't take much effort to rearrange the layout of the house to suit the occasion.

Solar panels use sunlight on the roof to generate electricity for the house.

Big windows give panoramic views in warm weather.

Rails on circular tracks form a perfectly level base for the various parts of the house to move on.

ROTATING HOUSE

▶▶ The D*Dynamic house is probably the strangest and coolest home you'll ever see. It can change shape to suit the weather! It is a rotating home designed for places that experience extreme temperatures—hot summers and freezing winters. During the cold winter months, it can be arranged as a square, with thick external walls and small windows to conserve heat. In summer, it opens up like a flower and turns inside out, with its glass panels facing outward to let in plenty of light.

Suite Vollard, Brazil

Dynamic buildings

Buildings that move are likely to become a more common part of city skylines in the future. A few have been built already. A building called Suite Vollard in Curitiba, Brazil, is the world's first rotating apartment building. Its circular floors rotate around a static core. Each floor takes an hour to go around once. The windows are tinted blue, gold, and silver, so the building is very eye-catching as the floors rotate in different directions.

⌄ HOW IT WORKS

▶▶ The house is divided into four parts shaped according to a formula worked out by the English mathematician Henry Ernest Dudeney. In 1908, he discovered that these four shapes can be arranged to make a perfect square and then rearranged to make a triangle. The parts of the house are linked together and stand on rails so that they can rotate around each other. As the building moves, doors transform into windows and internal walls become external walls. There are eight possible configurations of the house.

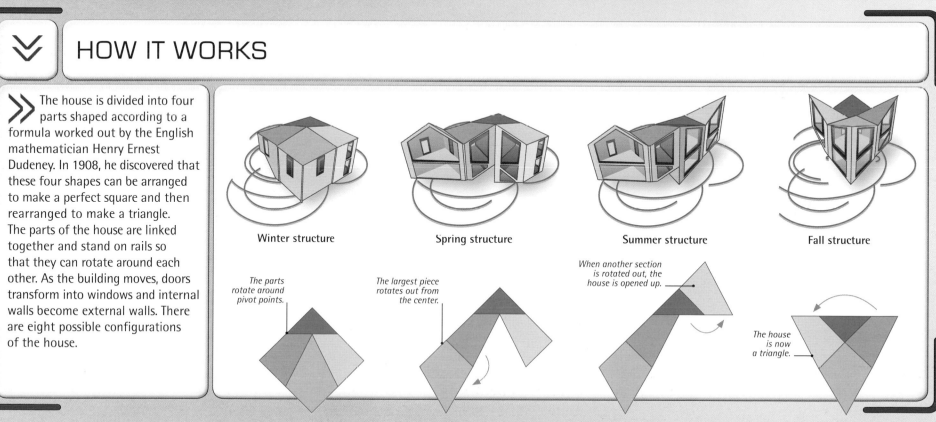

Winter structure

Spring structure

Summer structure

Fall structure

The parts rotate around pivot points.

The largest piece rotates out from the center.

When another section is rotated out, the house is opened up.

The house is now a triangle.

Water extracted from
the air collects in a
half-liter water bottle.

During a cycle, the Fontus device
cools the air whipping past in
order to release its water vapor.
In the right conditions, the unit
can produce half a liter (or about
a pint) of water in about an hour.

Water for
thirsty walkers

▲ There is a version of Fontus for
walkers. The cooling unit is built into
the bottle top, which also houses
a fan to draw in air. A flexible solar
panel wrapped around the bottle
charges the unit's battery.

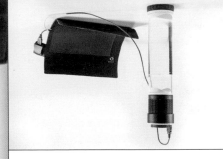

Fontus designed for walkers

FONTUS

▶▶ Water is essential for life. Access to clean, safe drinking water is a major issue for about 2 billion people around the world. A portable, solar-powered system called Fontus may just be the solution. The device collects the water vapor already present in the air and bottles it as a drinkable liquid. One version of Fontus is designed to fit on a bicycle, and it gradually refills itself with water during a ride.

Purifying water through pages

The Drinkable Book

Dirty water can make you very sick. The Drinkable Book was invented to help protect the health of millions of people who have no access to clean water. It works partly like an ordinary book, with printed pages explaining how to make water safe. The pages can be torn off and used as water filters. When dirty water is poured through a page, the paper filters out impurities and waterborne diseases. The folded paper, shown here lining the inside of a bucket, is suitable for use in rural households in developing countries.

HOW IT WORKS

▶▶ The Fontus system works by using solar power to cool down warm, humid air. It uses a cooler containing a device known as a Peltier element. When an electric current flows through the element, the bottom side heats up and the top side cools down—and cooling the hot side makes the cold side even colder. As the bike moves along at speed, air passes over the Peltier element and cools down. The moisture in the air condenses, forming water droplets that run down into the bottle, ready for collection.

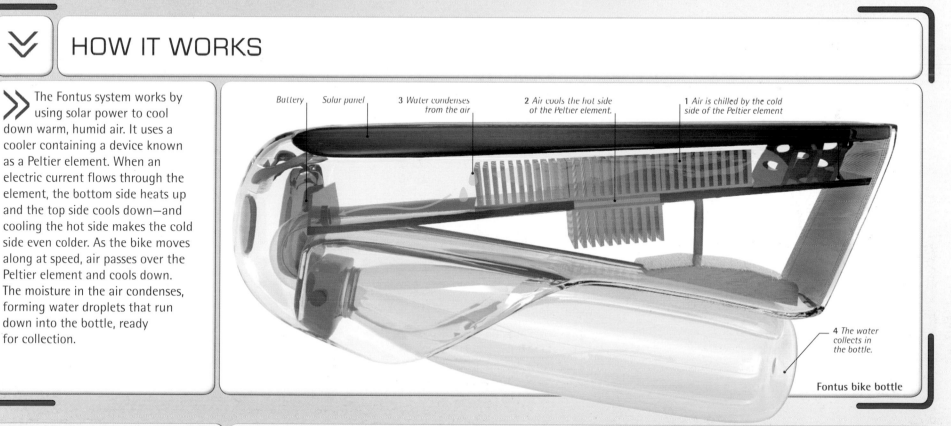

Battery   Solar panel   3 Water condenses from the air   2 Air cools the hot side of the Peltier element.   1 Air is chilled by the cold side of the Peltier element

4 The water collects in the bottle.

Fontus bike bottle

Electronic paper close-up

This false-color scanning electron microscope (SEM) image shows a rupture in electronic paper, the screen technology used in e-readers. The green lumps are charged e-ink particles, which are arranged into recognizable patterns of text or simple pictures using an electric field.

E-READER

▶▶ Using an e-reader is an alternative way to read a book. It is small and light enough to hold like a book, but unlike a book, it will never run out of text. When you finish one story, you can simply load or download another. The e-reader's screen displays words in the text from books using e-ink, which works in the same way as physical ink: We can see it because it reflects light from its surroundings. This is different than the screens of a tablet computer or smartphone, which produce their own light and can be tiring to look at for long periods.

E-reader advantages

As well being able to download and store many books, e-readers have other advantages over paper. Many e-readers can be controlled by touch, with the ability to make notes and send text to friends a standard feature. The size of the e-ink text can be adjusted to suit a reader's eyesight, and the typeface can also be changed. The latest e-readers also have small LEDs located at the edge of the screen that are pointed toward the screen. These light the text from the front (not the back like a computer screen), enabling the device to be read in the dark.

Pacey's Luck

Not many people know the story of Charlie Pacey—perhaps the most unique person I've ever had the honor of meeting. Every morning he got up, had a full breakfast, and left the house before the sparrows were up...

kindle

Touch screen e-reader

HOW IT WORKS

▶▶ E-ink devices display text using patterns of black and white dots made by particles inside oil-filled microcapsules. Each microcapsule is the width of a hair, and there are nearly 800,000 of them sandwiched between the transparent screen surface and an electrode. The e-reader sends an instruction in the form of an electric charge to every microcapsule each time the page is changed, causing the ink to show or disappear.

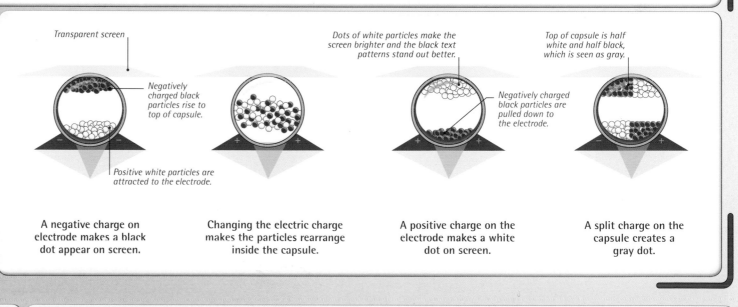

Transparent screen

Negatively charged black particles rise to top of capsule.

Positive white particles are attracted to the electrode.

Dots of white particles make the screen brighter and the black text patterns stand out better.

Negatively charged black particles are pulled down to the electrode.

Top of capsule is half white and half black, which is seen as gray.

A negative charge on electrode makes a black dot appear on screen.

Changing the electric charge makes the particles rearrange inside the capsule.

A positive charge on the electrode makes a white dot on screen.

A split charge on the capsule creates a gray dot.

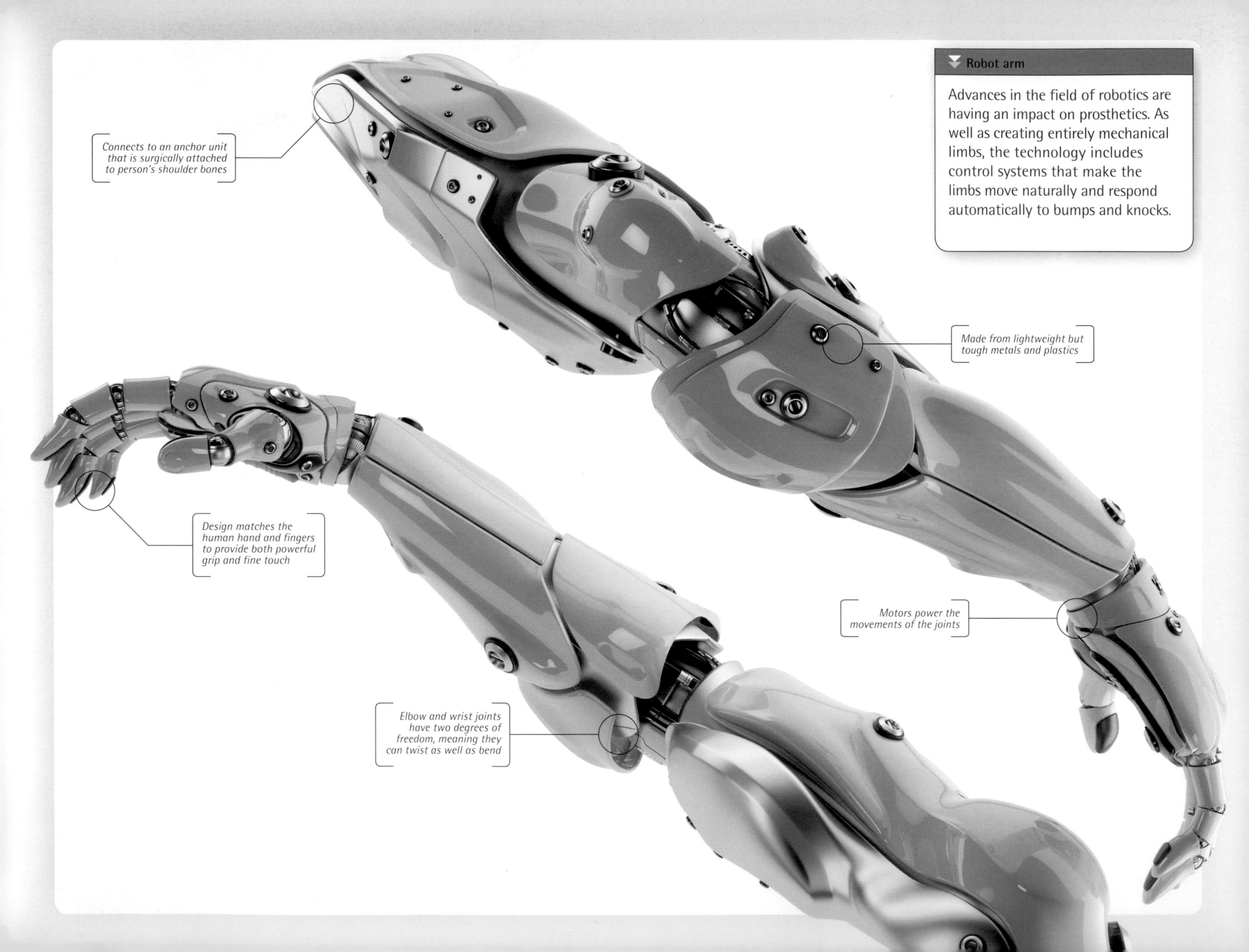

Connects to an anchor unit that is surgically attached to person's shoulder bones

Advances in the field of robotics are having an impact on prosthetics. As well as creating entirely mechanical limbs, the technology includes control systems that make the limbs move naturally and respond automatically to bumps and knocks.

Made from lightweight but tough metals and plastics

Design matches the human hand and fingers to provide both powerful grip and fine touch

Motors power the movements of the joints

Elbow and wrist joints have two degrees of freedom, meaning they can twist as well as bend

BIONIC
LIMBS

▶▶ People have been wearing prosthetics, or replacement body parts, for centuries. One of the oldest is a wooden toe used in ancient Egypt about 3,200 years ago. However, the latest technology is going far beyond such simple supports. Modern prosthetics can be controlled by brain impulses, meaning that wearers can learn to move them naturally, almost like a real limb.

⌄ Össur

▶▶ At the forefront of prosthetic limb technology is the Icelandic company Össur, who created the world's first bionic limb—a mechanical version of a biological leg, able to move under its own power. This Symbionic Leg attaches to the femur (thigh bone) of the upper leg, and has a knee joint, lower leg, ankle, and foot.

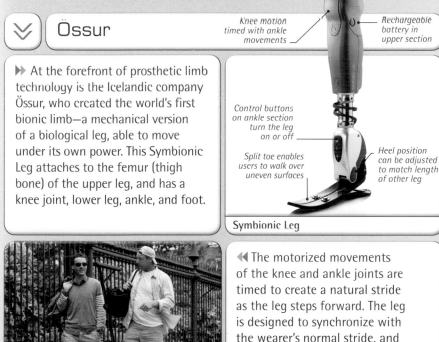

Knee motion timed with ankle movements

Rechargeable battery in upper section

Control buttons on ankle section turn the leg on or off

Split toe enables users to walk over uneven surfaces

Heel position can be adjusted to match length of other leg

Symbionic Leg

Walking using the Symbionic Leg

◀◀ The motorized movements of the knee and ankle joints are timed to create a natural stride as the leg steps forward. The leg is designed to synchronize with the wearer's normal stride, and to be treated like any other part of the body in terms of how the wearer moves and thinks of it, after a little practice.

⌄ HOW IT WORKS

▶▶ A bionic leg's movements are controlled by nerve signals from the brain, similar to the way a normal biological leg is controlled. The wearer must spend time learning how to think the bionic leg into action, but with practice, it is possible for that action to become more or less subconscious.

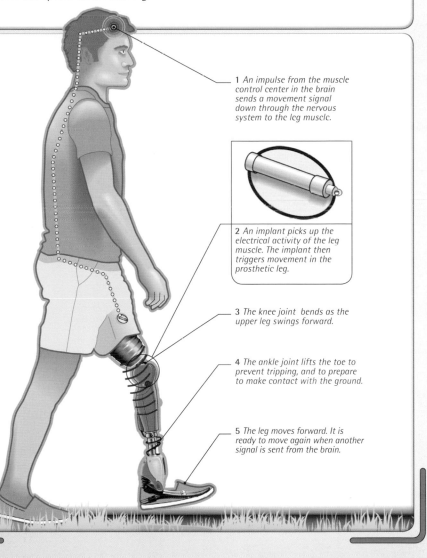

1 An impulse from the muscle control center in the brain sends a movement signal down through the nervous system to the leg muscle.

2 An implant picks up the electrical activity of the leg muscle. The implant then triggers movement in the prosthetic leg.

3 The knee joint bends as the upper leg swings forward.

4 The ankle joint lifts the toe to prevent tripping, and to prepare to make contact with the ground.

5 The leg moves forward. It is ready to move again when another signal is sent from the brain.

The sensors are housed in the underside of the drone.

The propeller is driven by a battery-powered electric motor.

The aircraft has a wingspan of 4 ft (1.2 m).

PRECISIC

◄ Lancaster drone

As a PrecisionHawk drone flies over the countryside, its sensors scan the ground. They can cover a large area faster than someone surveying the land on foot. The sensors can also see things that are not visible to the human eye.

COMMERCIAL
DRONE

 An unmanned aerial vehicle (UAV), also known as a drone, is a sort of flying robot that carries out work for its operator. While drones have been mostly utilized for military purposes, commercial drones have begun to be used by people working in fields such as farming, mining, oil drilling, forestry, and even search and rescue, by collecting all sorts of information from the air. American company PrecisionHawk's Lancaster UAV is one such craft. Though packed with cameras and sensors, it is light enough and small enough to be launched by hand. It can stay airborne for 45 minutes and fly at 25 mph (40 kph) at altitudes of up to 9,840 ft (3,000 m).

HOW IT WORKS

PrecisionHawk's Lancaster drone can survey an area of up to 300 acres (120 hectares) in one flight. It can also keep in contact with its operator up to a maximum of 12.4 miles (20 km) away.

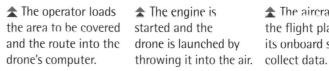
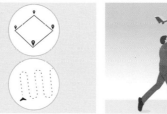

⏶ The operator loads the area to be covered and the route into the drone's computer.

⏶ The engine is started and the drone is launched by throwing it into the air.

⏶ The aircraft follows the flight plan while its onboard sensors collect data.

⏶ The data is sent to the operator for further processing and presentation.

Sensor types

The Lancaster drone can be fitted with different sensors, depending on the needs of the customer. On top of providing detailed images and video of the area being surveyed, the drone can scan the land using special sensors, and collect different data.

Fixed multispectral

Thermal

Selectable multispectral

LiDAR

⏶ Fixed multispectral sensors map the area, looking at the land through a specific part of the electromagnetic spectrum.

⏶ Thermal images map the heat energy given out by animals or humans on the ground—useful for search-and-rescue missions.

⏶ Using different filters, multispectral sensors can provide information on things like plant health, numbers, and water quality.

⏶ LiDAR (Light Detection and Ranging) uses a laser to make a high-resolution, 3-D map of the surface.

Garmin vívofit2

The display shows the number of steps made that day.

▲ This Garmin vívofit2 activity tracker is programmed to set daily activity goals for its wearer, based on his or her past fitness level. A red bar appears on the display when the wearer has been sitting down for an hour or more. Taking a short walk will clear that alert.

Activity trackers are crammed with sensors that measure all sorts of things—such as your speed, heart rate, physical position, and altitude. The real magic happens with the software that takes this information to build a profile of your activity.

ACTIVITY
TRACKER

▶▶ An activity tracker is a fitness aid that can help people maintain healthy exercise levels. Mostly worn on the wrist, or clipped to clothing, the tracker detects a person's motion. That data is combined with personal information, such as age, height, and weight, by the tracker's software to create a picture of a person's overall health and exercise levels. Activity trackers calculate how many calories a person has burned each day, which is useful information for people wanting to lose weight and keep fit. Some trackers worn against the skin can also measure heart rate, by detecting tiny color changes in the skin as the blood surges through it.

Wristify bracelet

Cooling bracelet

This Wristify device helps keep the body at a comfortable temperature. The gadget is still in development, but it is being designed to make use of a simple trick to cool, or warm, the body. It directs cool air onto the wrist, which chills the skin there. This makes the whole body seem to cool down so the wearer feels more comfortable. The bracelet will glow blue when cooling, or orange when providing a warming effect.

⌄ HOW IT WORKS

▲ Trackers can record sleep length and quality by recording movement as you sleep. This information can help you get more from your rest.

▲ Trackers sync their data to smartphone apps, usually via Bluetooth. The apps make it possible to analyze the data to see how you're doing.

▲ The easiest way to measure activity is by counting a person's footsteps. Motion sensors in the trackers can determine the rhythm and speed of your steps.

▲ Optical sensors in some trackers can detect the rate of blood flow through the skin. Heart rate data is used to show how hard you are working during exercise.

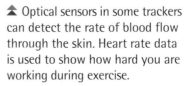

▲ Some trackers allow you to show your intended route on their screen, and use the Global Positioning System (GPS) to show where you are on a map.

The Panono photographs things around it using 36 cameras. To get the best view, the device is thrown straight up. Each camera takes a shot in the same instant, and they are stitched together into a single image that can be viewed via an app.

PANONO

▶▶ The Panono is a digital camera that takes pin-sharp images of everything in every direction to create a spherical 360-degree panorama. The 17-oz (480-g) camera can be held in the hand or on a selfie stick, but for best results it should be thrown into the air. An onboard accelerometer tracks the camera's trajectory and takes the photos at the highest point. The images are then viewed through an app, which displays the scene in every direction.

Swallowable camera

Edible camera

When a doctor needs to look at someone's digestive system, he or she can use a new type of camera. The device is the size of a large pill, and therefore small enough to swallow. Once inside, the camera lights up your insides using powerful LEDs, then records what it sees on video—all the way through to the other end. Once out, the video is available for download, giving the doctor useful clues as to what's wrong.

HOW IT WORKS

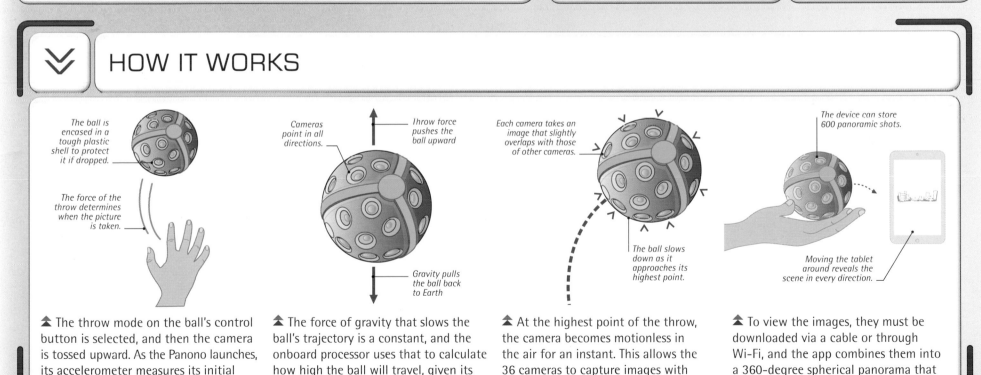

The ball is encased in a tough plastic shell to protect it if dropped.

The force of the throw determines when the picture is taken.

Cameras point in all directions.

Throw force pushes the ball upward

Gravity pulls the ball back to Earth

Each camera takes an image that slightly overlaps with those of other cameras.

The ball slows down as it approaches its highest point.

The device can store 600 panoramic shots.

Moving the tablet around reveals the scene in every direction.

⬆ The throw mode on the ball's control button is selected, and then the camera is tossed upward. As the Panono launches, its accelerometer measures its initial speed and direction.

⬆ The force of gravity that slows the ball's trajectory is a constant, and the onboard processor uses that to calculate how high the ball will travel, given its launch speed.

⬆ At the highest point of the throw, the camera becomes motionless in the air for an instant. This allows the 36 cameras to capture images with the minimum of blur.

⬆ To view the images, they must be downloaded via a cable or through Wi-Fi, and the app combines them into a 360-degree spherical panorama that really captures the whole scene.

Getting there

⏶ The first humans on Mars will arrive on a NASA Orion spacecraft. Orion, designed for traveling in deep space, will have a manned test flight in 2021.

Growing greens

⏶ Astronauts on Mars will grow fresh vegetables in a "space garden" like this. They will take fertilizer from Earth to add to the nutrient-poor Martian soil.

⏶ Building a Martian base

Conditions on Mars are lethal to humans, so manned Martian outposts will be safe shelters on a dangerous world. The atmosphere is unbreathable and extremely cold, and the planet is bombarded with deadly radiation from space.

A base built from Martian soil could protect pioneer settlers from deadly radiation.

LIVING ON
MARS

▶▶ People could be living on Mars, the "Red Planet," by the 2030s. A typical Mars mission will take about three years, longer than any human has been away from Earth before. After a flight lasting six to eight months, astronauts will spend about 500 days on Martian soil before their journey home. Their base camp buildings, the spacesuits they will wear, and the vehicles they will use for exploration are all currently being developed and tested.

An ISS astronaut works out

Staying healthy

Traveling to Mars and living on the planet could pose serious health risks for astronauts. One major problem is the low gravity on Mars. Without normal Earth gravity to work against, the human body loses muscle tone and bones become weaker. The best remedy is vigorous daily exercise, which astronauts on the International Space Station know all too well. They spend up to two hours a day working out on various exercise machines—running, cycling, and lifting weights.

ASTRONAUTS ON MARS—ON SCHEDULE

The NASA-planned journey to Mars has three phases. The Earth Reliant Phase, lasting up to the 2020s, is already underway. This stage involves research by the International Space Station into equipment and the effects of long spaceflights on the human body. During the Proving Ground Phase (2020s), missions will go as far as the moon to test the Mars spacecraft and other technology. Finally, the Earth Independent Phase (2030s) will use the moon's surface as a base for trials of the buildings and techniques that will be used for life on Mars.

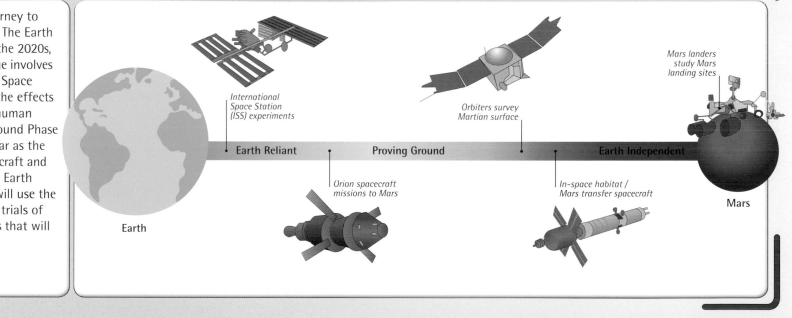

International
Space Station
(ISS) experiments

Orbiters survey
Martian surface

Mars landers
study Mars
landing sites

Earth Reliant   Proving Ground   Earth Independent

Orion spacecraft
missions to Mars

In-space habitat /
Mars transfer spacecraft

Earth

Mars

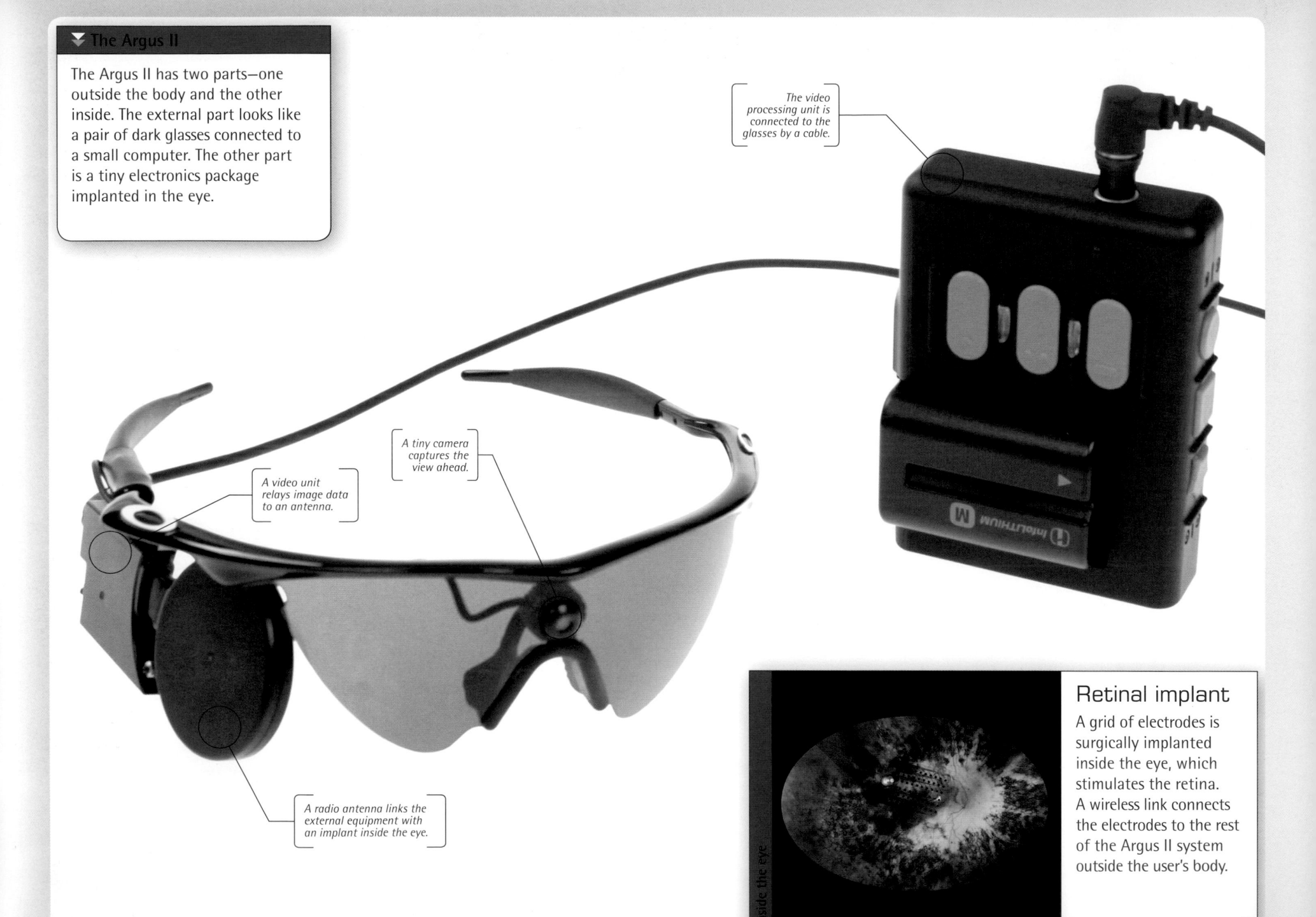

The Argus II

The Argus II has two parts—one outside the body and the other inside. The external part looks like a pair of dark glasses connected to a small computer. The other part is a tiny electronics package implanted in the eye.

The video processing unit is connected to the glasses by a cable.

A tiny camera captures the view ahead.

A video unit relays image data to an antenna.

A radio antenna links the external equipment with an implant inside the eye.

Inside the eye

Retinal implant

A grid of electrodes is surgically implanted inside the eye, which stimulates the retina. A wireless link connects the electrodes to the rest of the Argus II system outside the user's body.

SECOND SIGHT

▶▶ The Argus II is an implant designed to restore some sensation of sight to blind individuals. In a healthy eye, the lens focuses light onto the retina at the back of the eyeball, which in turn converts the light into electrical signals that the brain decodes as images. Reduced sight or even blindness can occur if the retina is damaged. The Argus II seeks to compensate for this non-fucntioning part of the eye.

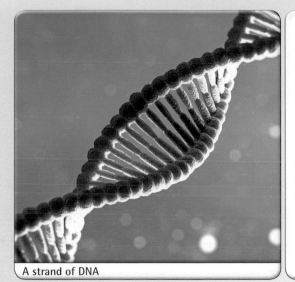
A strand of DNA

Personal medicine
Your DNA contains your unique genetic code, which tells every part of your body what to do. In the future, it's possible that DNA could be used to treat illnesses, with doctors analyzing code and prescribing medicine that is tailored to treat the unique genetic profile of their patients.

⌄ HOW IT WORKS

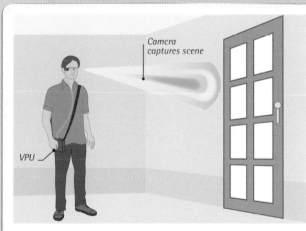

Camera captures scene

VPU

⤒ A tiny camera mounted in the middle of the eyeglasses captures the scene in front of the wearer and converts it into an electrical signal. This is sent to the video processing unit (VPU), which prepares it for the implant.

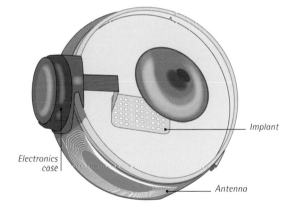

Implant

Electronics case

Antenna

⤒ The processed video signal is sent to a radio transmitter antenna mounted on the side of the glasses. The transmitted signal is picked up by a receiver attached to the eye and relayed to the implant inside the eye.

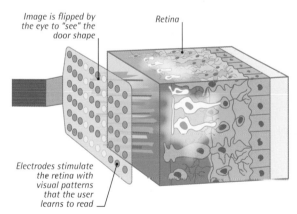

Image is flipped by the eye to "see" the door shape

Retina

Electrodes stimulate the retina with visual patterns that the user learns to read

⤒ The processed video signal is sent to a grid of 60 electrodes inside the eye. The electrodes stimulate the retina's remaining working cells. They pass the signal down the optic nerve to the brain, which enables you to see spots of lights.

Prevention

While the Ocean Cleanup project removes plastic trash already in the ocean, it's important to prevent more plastic from getting into the ocean in the first place. A lot of it is washed down rivers from cities. Floating booms similar to Ocean Cleanup's barriers are already being used in some river mouths to trap garbage.

Plastic pollution

A platform extracts the plastic and stores it for collection and removal.

Wind and currents carry plastic toward a floating barrier.

Plastic debris builds up behind the barrier.

▶▶ Testing floating barriers

The Ocean Cleanup's barriers have been tested in the North Sea, collecting balls instead of garbage. The next step is to test them in the ocean. A 6,562-ft (2,000-m) long barrier will be installed in the Tsushima Strait off the coast of Japan in 2016.

THE OCEAN
CLEANUP PROJECT

▶▶ Every year, millions of tons of plastic waste enters the world's oceans. Ultraviolet radiation breaks it down into smaller and smaller pieces by a process called photodegradation. This plastic pollution isn't just ugly; it's dangerous. The chemicals it contains harm the creatures that eat the plastic. The Ocean Cleanup project aims to collect this plastic and remove it from the oceans by using specially designed floating barriers.

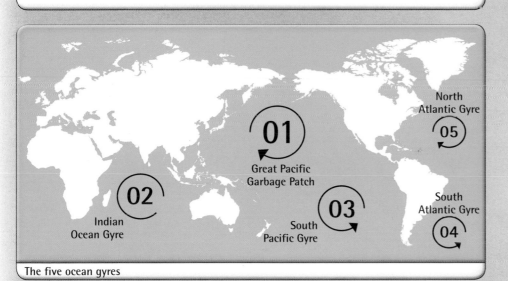

North Atlantic Gyre

01

Great Pacific Garbage Patch

05

02

Indian Ocean Gyre

South Pacific Gyre

03

South Atlantic Gyre

04

The five ocean gyres

Ocean gyres

The ocean currents that concentrate plastic pollution at sea are called gyres. There are five of them. They flow around and around in circles, trapping floating trash in the middle. A third of all the plastic in the oceans is trapped in the biggest gyre. It's called the Great Pacific Garbage Patch, and it's located in the North Pacific Gyre between the west coast of the United States and Japan. About 80 percent of the debris it contains came from land, and the rest was dumped by ships.

⌄ HOW IT WORKS

Garbage collects here.

Floating barriers trap plastic

◀◀ A V-shaped array of long floating barriers will catch plastic pollution. These barriers don't need to move to collect the plastic. In fact, they are anchored to the ocean floor. Nature will do the work. The barriers will be placed in locations where ocean currents will carry the plastic toward them.

▶▶ Not all of the plastic pollution in the ocean floats. Some of it is suspended below the surface. Screens hanging down under the booms will gather this subsurface plastic. Most of the water current will pass under these screens. Fish and other sea creatures will also be able to swim under the screens.

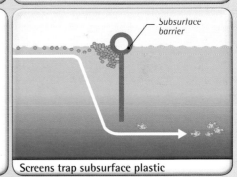

Subsurface barrier

Screens trap subsurface plastic

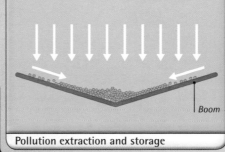

Boom

Pollution extraction and storage

◀◀ The V shape of the barriers is the key to their operation. Once plastic is trapped behind a barrier, ocean currents will move it toward the point of the V, where a central platform will extract the plastic. It will then be stored on-site until it can be transported to land for recycling or disposal.

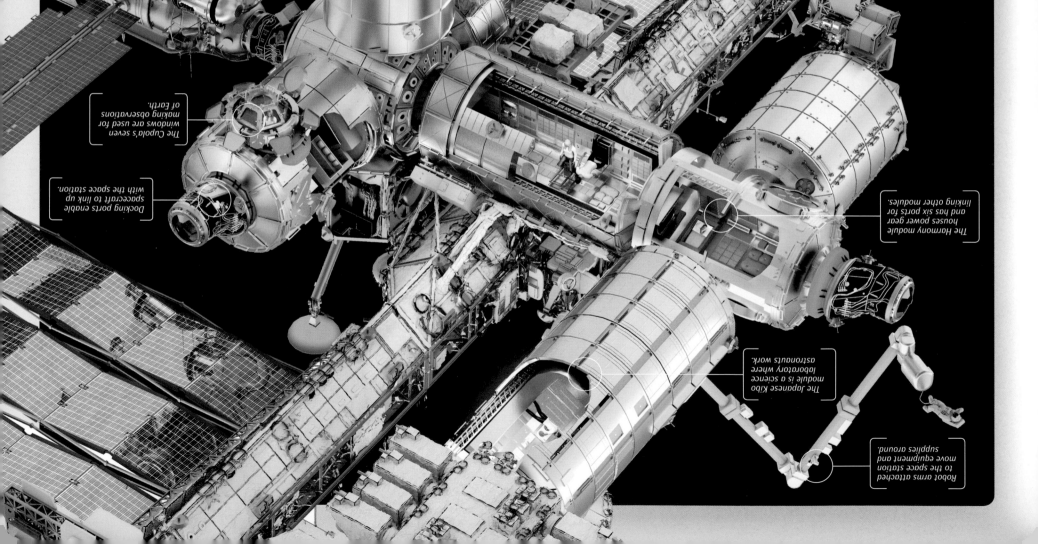

Astronauts spend about 35 hours each week conducting research and experiments in the spacecraft's weightless environment. The station travels at a speed of 5 miles (7.6 km) a second, and completes an orbit of Earth every 90 minutes.

The Cupola's seven windows are used for making observations of Earth.

Docking ports enable spacecraft to link up with the space station.

The Harmony module houses power gear and has six ports for linking other modules.

The Japanese Kibo module is a science laboratory where astronauts work.

Robot arms attached to the space station move equipment and supplies around.

LIVING IN THE ISS

▶▶ The International Space Station (ISS) is a space laboratory that was assembled, piece by piece, 250 miles (400 km) above the surface of Earth. It has been continuously occupied since 2000, and in that time, more than 200 astronauts from 15 countries have worked in its weightless environment. These astronauts conduct research to advance our understanding of science—from how humans can live in space to how to prepare for exploration beyond Earth.

The giant in space

The ISS is the biggest and costliest structure ever built in space. It's the size of a soccer field, and its cost is estimated at around $100 billion.

On Earth, it would weigh 930,000 lb (420,000 kg). It is powered by electricity generated by 27,000 ft² (2,500 m²) of solar panels.

ISS in orbit around Earth

⌄ Life on board

▶▶ The space station needs regular maintenance work and occasional repairs. Sometimes astronauts have to don spacesuits and go outside to do this work. ISS astronauts have made about 200 spacewalks.

Repairing the ISS

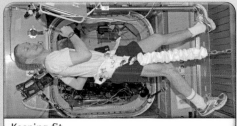
Keeping fit

◀◀ Daily exercise is vital to maintain the crew's health and fitness, and stave off the effects of weightlessness. The astronauts use an exercise bike and treadmill to help minimize muscle and bone loss.

▶▶ ISS astronauts carry out experiments in a variety of physical and biological sciences, including studies of plant growth. This is important because future astronauts will have to grow their own food.

Studying plant growth

Viewing Earth from the Cupola

◀◀ When the astronauts aren't working, they relax by reading, listening to music, and watching movies. They also like to spend time watching Earth through the Cupola's windows, the largest fitted to any spacecraft.

MEDICAL MARVELS

Medical science tends to be at the forefront of technology as small advances can help cure diseases and save lives. The miniaturization of electronics means that computing devices may soon be working on or inside your body, and technology that takes control of the way a body grows will be able to replace body parts completely.

◄ Antivirus robots

DNA carries our genetic code in a precise sequence of chemical units. If a virus or illness invades the body, future biomedical engineers may be able to program new, non-genetic DNA molecules to be delivered to the affected parts of the body by tiny robots. The robots deliver their load and fix the problem, before decaying into harmless fragments.

◄ Biostamp tattoo

In future, doctors might use biostamps to monitor a patient's health. The temporary tattoo is an ultrathin microchip that is waterproof and able to move with the skin. The chip will send data on things like activity levels, hydration, and blood pressure via a wireless transmitter, giving doctors a better picture of how the patient's body is working over a couple of weeks.

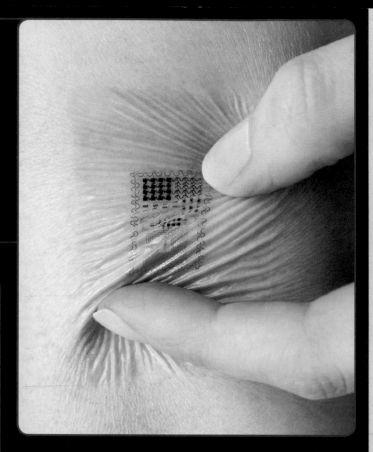

Model patient

SimMan is a robot patient used to teach nurses and doctors how to look after real people. Trainers can instruct it to speak, bleed, sweat, breathe in and out, urinate, and even cry. The robot can simulate the many different ways human patients need help from medical staff, giving them a valuable chance to practice without harming anyone if they get it wrong.

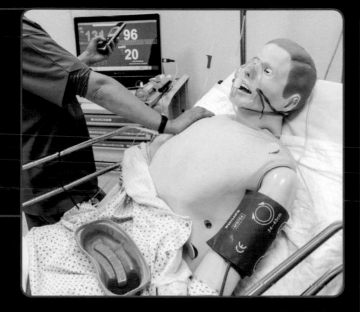

Organ growing

Researchers have learned how to grow extra kidneys inside lab rats, a process that could be scaled up to make it possible to grow new organs inside human bodies to replace damaged ones. The system requires special human body cells to be grown in the lab. These are then implanted into an adult body, where they continue to grow into a new organ.

Synthetic skin

A flexible plastic laced with silicon and gold is being developed as a touch-sensitive, synthetic skin. Tiny electronic sensors inside it can pick up pressure, heat, cold, and moisture, thus offering the same span of senses as human skin.

FUTURE 6

Some of the inventions in this chapter haven't been created yet. They are possible in theory—we just need to figure out how to make them work. Other concepts have already been realized. Artificial intelligence is already pretty sophisticated, and commuter drones are not science fiction—they exist. We will have to wait a little longer for flying cars, quantum computers, and teleportation machines. The future will be full of the coolest tech imaginable.

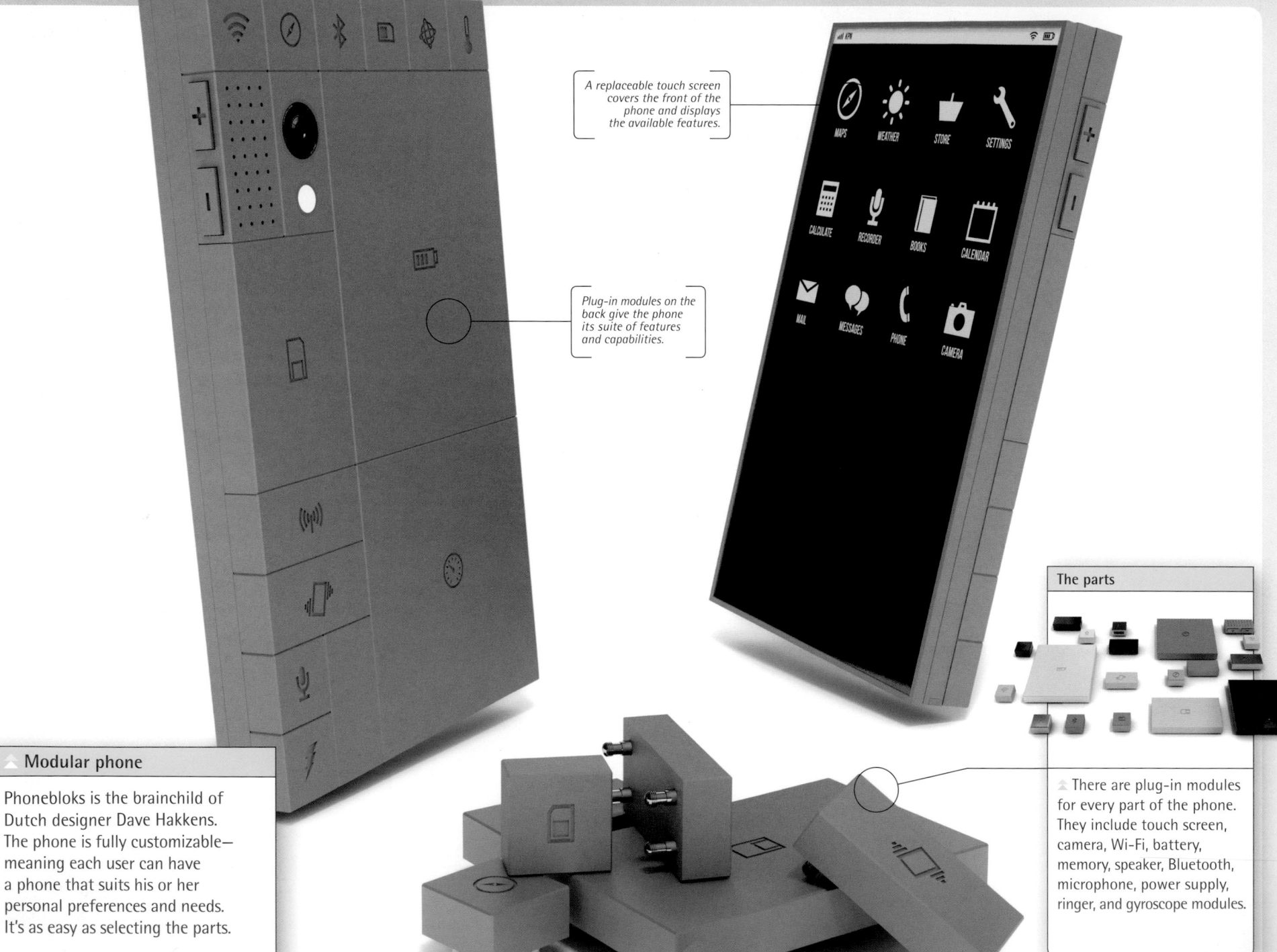

A replaceable touch screen covers the front of the phone and displays the available features.

Plug-in modules on the back give the phone its suite of features and capabilities.

MAPS · WEATHER · STORE · SETTINGS
CALCULATE · RECORDER · BOOKS · CALENDAR
MAIL · MESSAGES · PHONE · CAMERA

The parts

▲ Modular phone

Phonebloks is the brainchild of Dutch designer Dave Hakkens. The phone is fully customizable—meaning each user can have a phone that suits his or her personal preferences and needs. It's as easy as selecting the parts.

▲ There are plug-in modules for every part of the phone. They include touch screen, camera, Wi-Fi, battery, memory, speaker, Bluetooth, microphone, power supply, ringer, and gyroscope modules.

PHONEBLOKS

One of the most visible pieces of technology in our daily lives is the cell phone. But with most people changing their phone regularly to keep up with the latest technology, the disposal of old phones has created mountains of waste. A concept called Phonebloks seeks to reduce this waste by creating a phone made of separate pieces called modules that can be easily replaced.

Electronic waste

Hundreds of millions of cell phones are thrown away every year. They contain valuable materials that can be recovered. A million cell phones contain about 75 lb (34 kg) of gold, 770 lb (350 kg) of silver, 30 lb (15 kg) of palladium, and 35,000 lb (16,000 kg) of copper. Taiwanese artist Lin Shih-Pao built a car from 25,000 used cell phones to show how they can be recycled as art.

Lin Shih-Pao's installation

Phonebloks modules plug into a base, or motherboard. This connects the modules so they communicate with one another. Two screws lock everything together.

Users choose modules to suit their needs. For example, they might choose a basic phone camera or a more sophisticated camera module made by a camera manufacturer.

Modules have metal pins that plug into holes in the base.

Users create their own phone with the specific set of features they want.

Standard-sized, interchangeable modules fit every phone.

A bigger battery could be chosen by someone who might go longer without being able to charge their phone than most.

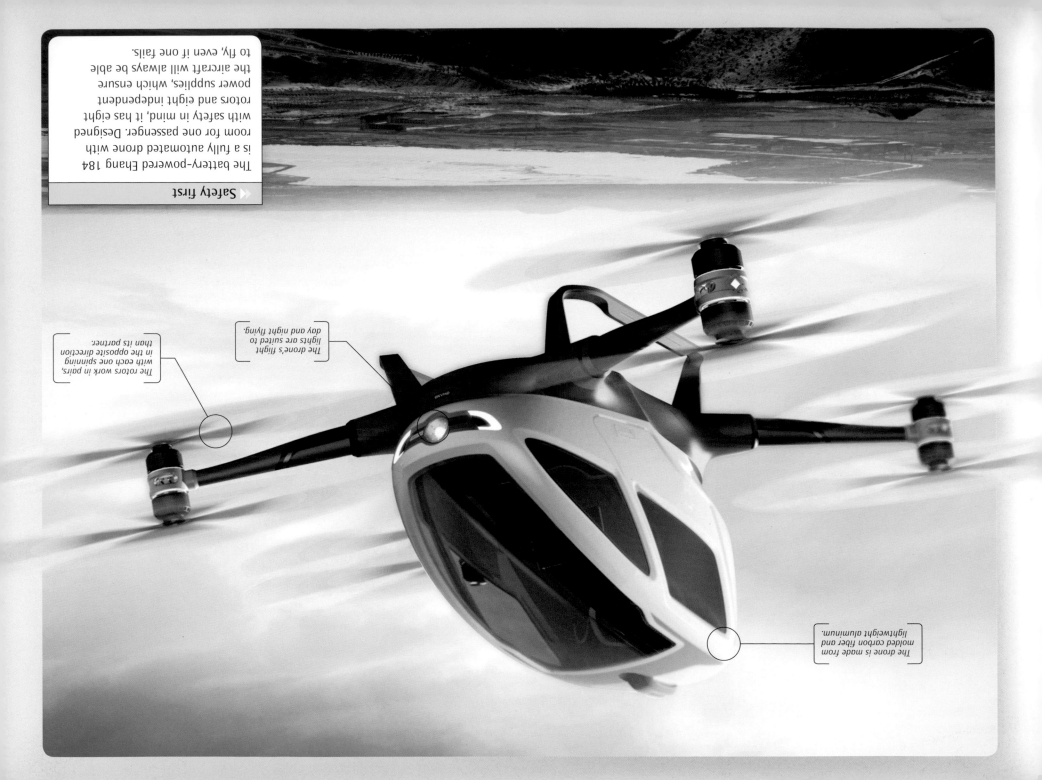

The rotors work in pairs, with each one spinning in the opposite direction than its partner.

The drone's flight lights are suited to day and night flying.

The drone is made from molded carbon fiber and lightweight aluminum.

PASSENGER
DRONE

Drones are uncrewed aircraft piloted by remote control or flying autonomously. The Ehang 184 is a drone with a difference: human cargo. This octocopter—so named for its eight independent rotors—has no pilot. Its passenger selects a flight plan and destination, and the drone does the rest, able to carry a person on a 20-minute flight at speeds of up to 62 mph (100 kph).

A droneport concept for Rwanda

Droneport

It is estimated that only one-third of Africans live within walking distance of an all-season road, which means that getting vital medical supplies to isolated communities is a huge problem. Rwanda, dubbed the "land of a thousand hills," has been selected as the location of the world's first droneport. It is hoped that automated long-distance drones, taking off from the droneport, will be able to go where roads don't, and take life-saving supplies to some of the most remote areas on Earth.

HOW IT WORKS

A tablet in the passenger cabin controls the Ehang's flight plan. This connects with a central server, which coordinates the journey with other aircraft in the area, overriding flight requests when flight conditions are poor. The drone follows an inverted U flight path, taking off and landing vertically and cruising at a constant altitude of 1,640 ft (500 m), using satellite data to navigate its flight path.

The passenger can check the status of the aircraft and control cabin conditions.

A live GPS map shows the drone's progress during the flight.

The drone control app runs on a normal tablet computer.

The passenger can decide to hover or land at any location.

Researchers at the University of Rochester in New York have succeeded in making things vanish. Unlike other invisibility systems, which rely on complex arrangements of cameras and mirrors, the Rochester system uses inexpensive lenses.

Part of the hand vanishes, but the background remains visible.

Lenses bend light around the hand.

BECOMING
INVISIBLE

Most people have probably wondered what it might be like to be invisible, but there is currently no way of making people disappear. That may not be the case for much longer, however, as scientists are trying to develop ways to make things invisible, and they've had some success. So far, these prototype invisibility systems work only under strictly controlled laboratory conditions, and for relatively small things. The next step is to take them out of the laboratory and make them work in the real world. If they are successful, you might be flitting by unseen before you know it!

What use is invisibility?

The ability to make someone or something invisible is interesting, but what use would it be? Imagine the view from an airliner with an invisible floor or walls. People who study wild animals and film them usually have to hide from view. Their work would be a lot easier if they could make themselves invisible.

African lioness in her natural habitat

Military forces are very interested in invisibility research. Stealth technology has rendered aircraft such as the B-2 stealth bomber virtually undetectable by radar. Imagine how much more difficult it would be to fight against soldiers, tanks, or aircraft if they could be made more difficult to see or even invisible on the battlefield.

B-2 bomber

HOW IT WORKS

The University of Rochester's invisibility system relies on the ability of lenses to bend light. One lens concentrates a background image into a narrow beam. Two more lenses stop the beam from expanding until it reaches the fourth lens, which restores the image to its original size. Anything placed outside the narrow beam (the cloaked region) will not be seen through the fourth lens.

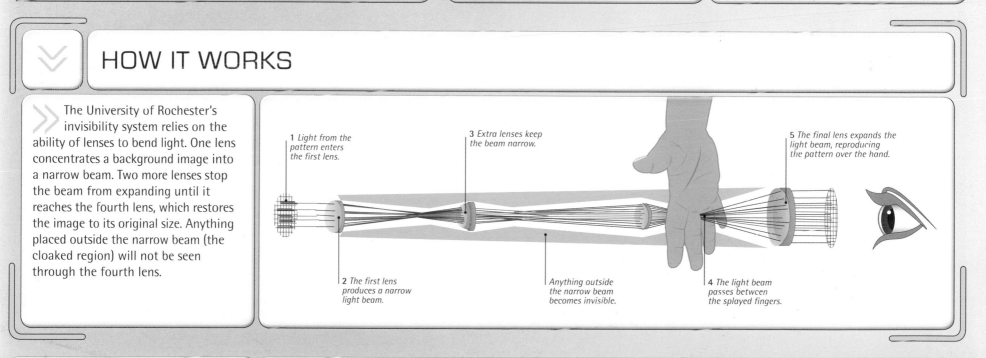

1 Light from the pattern enters the first lens.

2 The first lens produces a narrow light beam.

3 Extra lenses keep the beam narrow.

Anything outside the narrow beam becomes invisible.

4 The light beam passes between the splayed fingers.

5 The final lens expands the light beam, reproducing the pattern over the hand.

SPACE FRONTIERS

The new rockets and spacecraft that will be needed to help us explore further in space are already being built and tested. Engineers are also thinking about how to do things that seem impossible today. It is possible that faster-than-light galactic travel, elevators reaching to space, and hibernating astronauts will all become reality.

▲ SLS

NASA is developing the world's most powerful rocket for launching craft carrying astronauts and cargo into orbit. Called the Space Launch System (SLS), its first flight is scheduled for the end of 2018. SLS will be able to lift more than 143 tons (130 metric tons)—more than the weight of 85 family cars—and take people farther into space than ever before.

▼ Space tether

An unusual idea for moving spacecraft in space is to use a long cable known as a space tether. As a spacecraft passes through a planet's magnetic field, electricity flows along the tether. The energy could perhaps be channeled as a fuel-saving power. A rotating tether might also be used to catch a spacecraft and catapult it into higher orbit.

▶▶ Warp drive

To travel faster than light, starships in movies are said to have the ability to expand the space behind them and contract the space in front of them. Scientifically speaking, the idea could potentially work, but we currently do not have the ability to do it. If we could find a way, it would allow us to venture farther in our universe than we could even imagine now.

◀◀ Space elevator

Imagine riding an elevator from Earth into space. Engineers suggest that such a creation could be made of super-strong carbon ribbons, anchored to the ground and extending 62,000 miles (100,000 km) into space. Elevator cars would climb up the ribbons into space.

▶▶ Sleeper craft

For long space flights to Mars and beyond, NASA is investigating the possibility of putting astronauts into a deep sleep called torpor, similar to hibernation in animals. This might be done by lowering the astronauts' body temperature. They could then be woken on arrival.

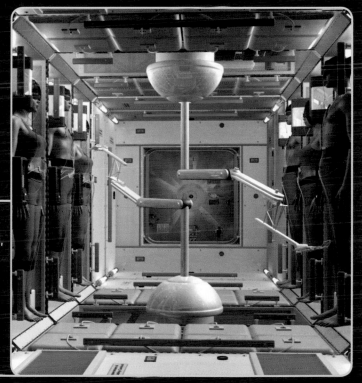

Super fast travel

Hyperloop will whisk passengers from city to city faster than a jet airliner. You may not be able to enjoy the view, though, because the capsules will travel inside tubes. Test tracks are being built to develop the concept's technology.

Most of the air is sucked out of the tunnel to enable the capsule to travel faster.

The Hyperloop's streamlined body slips through the remaining air in the tunnel easily.

Hyperloop has no wheels. Instead, it rides on top of a thin cushion of air.

HYPERLOOP

Imagine taking a trip at speeds of 760 mph (1,220 kph). You could go from San Francisco, California, to Los Angeles, California—a journey that normally takes nearly six hours by car—in only 30 minutes. The extraordinary vehicle that could make this possible is called the Hyperloop. Passengers will sit in capsules inside a tube that serves as the track. A combination of magnets, electricity, and air causes the capsule to zip by. Each section of the tube is flexible, meaning it is earthquake-proof, and the capsules are prevented from bumping into one another other by air pressure.

HOW IT WORKS

A Hyperloop capsule will be propelled by electromagnetic motors. When an electric current is applied, magnets in the capsule and track cause the capsule to move forward. A fan sucks in air from the front of the capsule, and blows most of it backward behind it. Some of it is blown downward to create a cushion that supports the capsule instead of wheels, like a puck on an air hockey table.

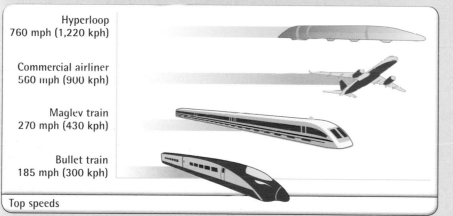

Hyperloop
760 mph (1,220 kph)

Commercial airliner
560 mph (900 kph)

Maglev train
270 mph (430 kph)

Bullet train
185 mph (300 kph)

Top speeds

Comparing speeds

Hyperloop aims to combine the speed of air transportation, or even faster speeds, with the convenience of rail travel. Its average speed would be about 600 mph (965 kph)—a little faster than an airliner's cruising speed. At this speed, it would be three times faster than a Japanese bullet train, and it would easily win a race against the current rail speed record holder in passenger service, the Shanghai Maglev Train (SMT).

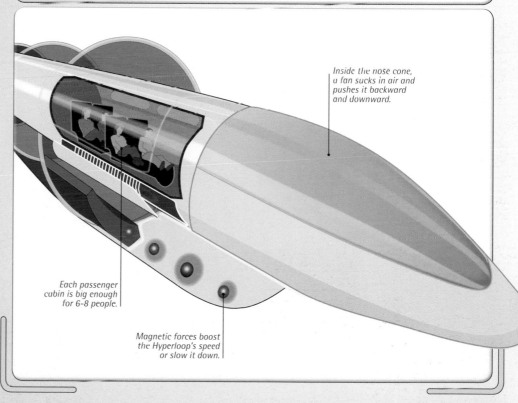

Inside the nose cone, a fan sucks in air and pushes it backward and downward.

Each passenger cabin is big enough for 6-8 people.

Magnetic forces boost the Hyperloop's speed or slow it down.

▶ Arriving safely

Teleportation is not so much traveling as communication between two points—only the message in this case is your whole body. The possibility of being able to go on a faraway vacation in seconds is a long way off, but may be possible.

Traveler is inside teleporter

TELEPORTATION

▶▶ What would it be like to dematerialize in a teleporter? Would your thoughts, memories, and personality be teleported, along with the particles that make up your body? Would the teleported person really be "you" in every way? This may seem impossible, but scientists are actually carrying out research and experimentation in teleportation, and they've had some success. So far, only a tiny bit of light energy has been teleported this way, with a record distance currently of 89 miles (143 km). It might not be impossible after all!

⌄ HOW IT WORKS

▲ A traveler stands on a teleporter pod, which scans the traveler and maps the positions of all the matter in his body.

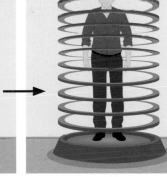

▲ Powerful scanning disrupts the atoms in the traveler's body and causes the person to dematerialize.

▲ The scan data is transmitted. It is received by another pod, which uses it to recreate, or materialize, the traveler.

⌄ Quantum leap

▶▶ Teleportation research uses something called quantum entanglement. Two particles or photons are entangled if they are synchronized so closely that altering one automatically alters the other, even if they are far apart. It enables scientists to teleport bits of quantum information (called qubits) in experiments.

Quantum entanglement

Teleportation may improve credit card security

▲ Long before it becomes possible to teleport people (if it ever does), quantum teleportation could lead to lightning-fast Internet services and better credit card security—because they both involve moving a lot of information quickly.

The oven can be controlled remotely or follow instructions from a recipe to come on at the right temperature and at the right time for each day's meals.

Lights come on automatically as a person approaches a room, using signals from his or her personal activity tracker. The lighting level adapts to the time of day and weather, as well as to activity such as eating, watching TV, or working.

Weather forecasts and sensors around the house are used to adjust the temperature inside the home to keep it at optimal levels for the time of day and the homeowner's preference.

As well as being used for watching television, the screens in the house are controllers for all the other systems in the home.

The refrigerator scans food to track what items are inside, how long they have been there, how often they are used, and how much is left.

A chip on your pet monitors its activity and location, giving a warning if it enters forbidden areas, and opening feeders when it is hungry.

Biometric locks on the exterior doors record who is currently in the house, and can be programmed to open to accept prearranged deliveries.

⬆ Internet at home

The Internet of Things will transform the home, connecting everyday devices together. They can all be operated remotely from central controllers, but these systems also share information and respond automatically to each other's actions.

INTERNET OF THINGS

>> There are more devices connected to the Internet than there are people on Earth. As this number increases, and the devices become interconnected, it will form the Internet of Things (IoT). The IoT will give people remote access to their house and office and allow them to interact in new ways with public spaces such as stores, tourist attractions, and transportation networks. The data collected by these devices will be used to build intelligent systems that help people live healthier and more efficient lives.

Traffic congestion

On the road
Outside the home, the IoT will revolutionize our everyday lives in interesting ways. Traffic jams may be a thing of the past, because the IoT takes up-to-the-minute information from all modes of transportation to keep you on the move. This data will then present you with the best routes around delays—but the IoT will not send everybody the same route, reducing the chances of further jams on alternative routes.

HOW IT WORKS

In the home, the IoT will work by coordinating smart devices and analyzing the behavior of their owner. This means that one system, such as a smart fridge, can learn to manage a person's groceries automatically, taking into consideration the habits of the owner. It can also attempt to improve the owner's health by suggesting solutions to simple problems, such as ordering healthier food for the refrigerator, or diagnosing an illness.

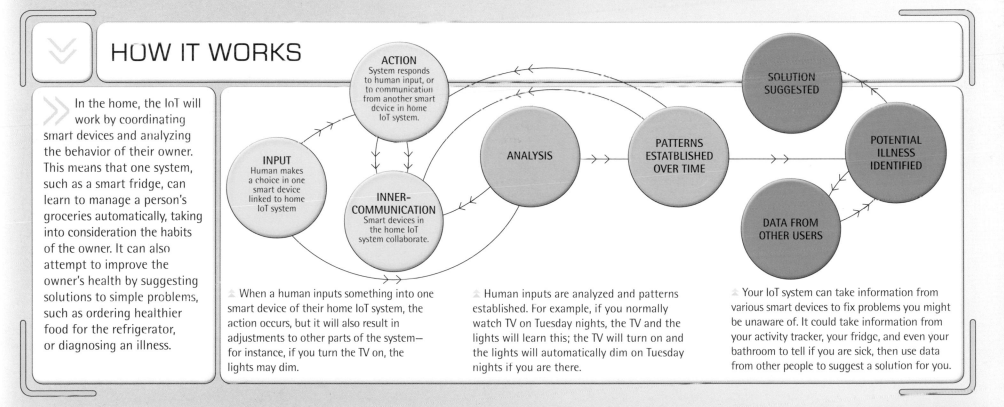

ACTION System responds to human input, or to communication from another smart device in home IoT system.

INPUT Human makes a choice in one smart device linked to home IoT system

INNER-COMMUNICATION Smart devices in the home IoT system collaborate.

ANALYSIS

PATTERNS ESTATBLISHED OVER TIME

SOLUTION SUGGESTED

POTENTIAL ILLNESS IDENTIFIED

DATA FROM OTHER USERS

⚊ When a human inputs something into one smart device of their home IoT system, the action occurs, but it will also result in adjustments to other parts of the system— for instance, if you turn the TV on, the lights may dim.

⚊ Human inputs are analyzed and patterns established. For example, if you normally watch TV on Tuesday nights, the TV and the lights will learn this; the TV will turn on and the lights will automatically dim on Tuesday nights if you are there.

⚊ Your IoT system can take information from various smart devices to fix problems you might be unaware of. It could take information from your activity tracker, your fridge, and even your bathroom to tell if you are sick, then use data from other people to suggest a solution for you.

Skype Translator is one example of an AI system. It enables people speaking in two different languages to have a conversation in real time. The translator recognizes what is said in one language and translates it into another, and back again.

नमस्ते मेरा नाम किंषुक है। आप कैसी हैं?

Hello, my name is Kingshuk. How are you?

Hello Kingshuk, I'm Smiljka. I'm in school. We are having a lesson about India. Where in the country do you live?

नमस्ते किंषुक। मेरा नाम स्मीका है। मैं स्कूल में हूँ। हम लोग इंडिया के बारे मे पढ़ रहे हैं। आप इंडिया में कहाँ रहते हैं?

मैं नई दिल्ली में रहता हूँ। मुझे यह जगह बहुत पसंद है। यह एक ऐतिहासिक शहर है और यहाँ का खाना काफ़ी स्वादिष्ट है। आप कहाँ रहती हैं?

I live in New Delhi. I really love it. This is a historic city and the food here is delicious. Where do you live?

I live near London. It's nice but it's very cold right now.

मैं लंदन के पास रहती हूँ। यह जगह अच्छी है मगर इस समय यहाँ बहुत सर्दी है।

Type a message in English here

ARTIFICIAL INTELLIGENCE

▶▶ Computers are getting better at acting like humans. As a result, artificial intelligence (AI) is progressing at an unprecedented rate, and often in areas you might not realize. AI systems are now able to diagnose diseases from a set of symptoms, play complex board games against human competitors, and translate speech from one language to another in real time. As an AI does these things and more, it learns from the things that happen afterward, much in the way that humans do—with each situation improving the AI system's understanding of future situations.

Man versus machine

The Turing Test

In 1950, the English mathematician Alan Turing developed a test to check whether or not a machine is intelligent. The test, which became known as the Turing Test, involves a person and a machine communicating with each other using text. If the person can't tell whether he or she is communicating with a machine or another person, then the machine has passed the test.

⌄ HOW IT WORKS

≫ AI-driven translators, such as Skype Translator, enable you to talk to your friends in real time, even if they do not speak the same language as you. The artificial intelligence at work here is the translator's ability to understand exactly what the speakers mean, which is determined by the translator breaking down the noises you make into small parts, and comparing them with known words in its Internet-linked database. It must be able to do this in a split second in order for a conversation to run smoothly.

"it's ah nice..."
"it's ah nice..."
"it's nice..."

⬆ When the first person speaks, the translator analyzes the sound and compares it to recorded audio snippets in its database to identify the words.

⬆ Any unnecessary sounds—such as *um*s, *ah*s, and repetitions—are removed from the speech; they are unimportant to its meaning.

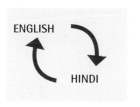

ENGLISH

HINDI

⬆ Skype Translator thenuses its artificially intelligent "knowledge" of languages to translate the words into the second person's language.

यह जगह अच्छी है मगर इस समय यहाँ बहुत सर्दी है।

⬆ The translated words are shown to the second person, and can be spoken by the program's voice generator. A response from the second person starts the cycle again.

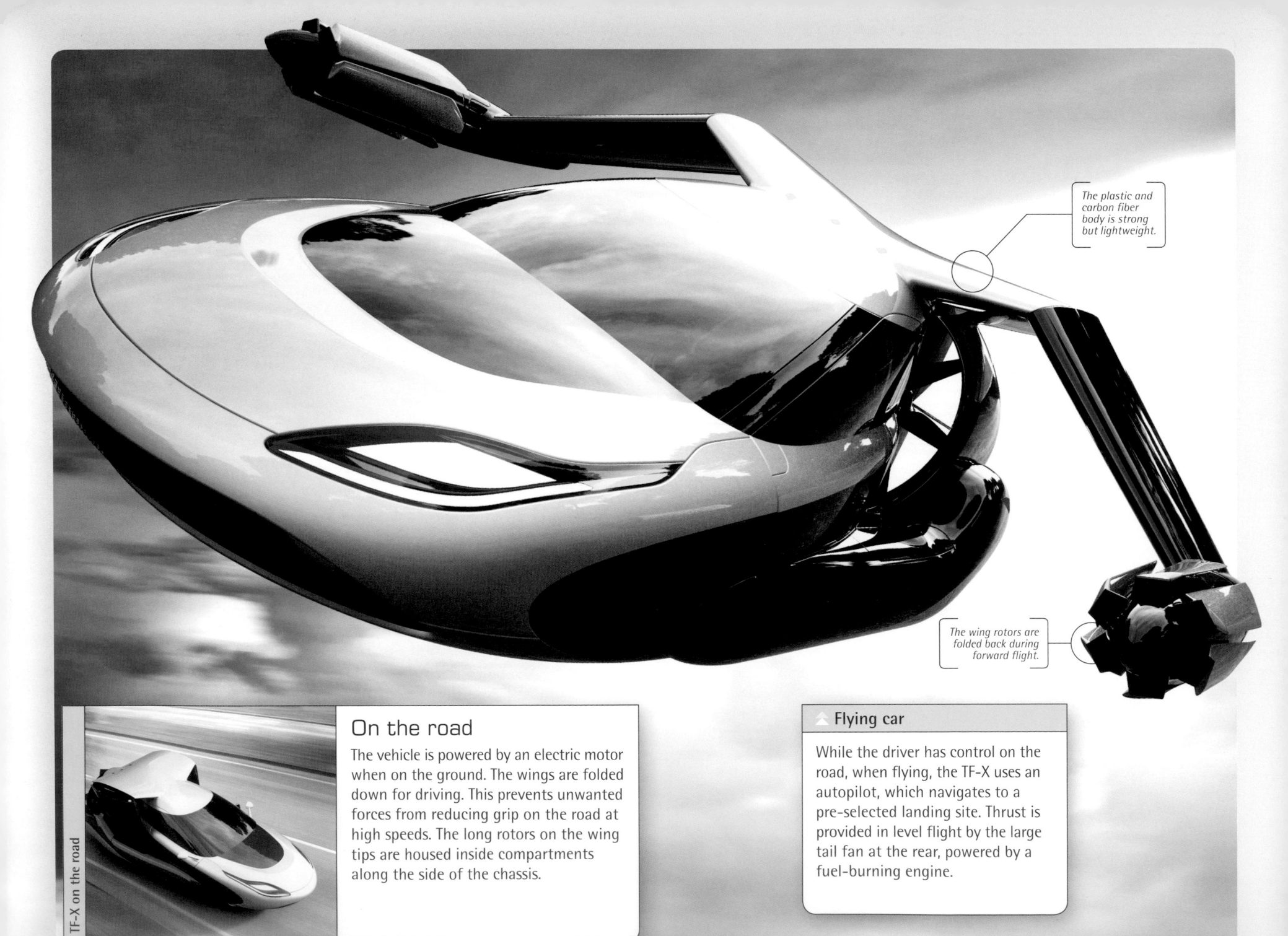

The plastic and carbon fiber body is strong but lightweight.

The wing rotors are folded back during forward flight.

TF-X on the road

On the road

The vehicle is powered by an electric motor when on the ground. The wings are folded down for driving. This prevents unwanted forces from reducing grip on the road at high speeds. The long rotors on the wing tips are housed inside compartments along the side of the chassis.

🔺 Flying car

While the driver has control on the road, when flying, the TF-X uses an autopilot, which navigates to a pre-selected landing site. Thrust is provided in level flight by the large tail fan at the rear, powered by a fuel-burning engine.

FLYING CAR

The future for the humble car is, perhaps, in the air. TF-X is a concept car designed to transform everyday journeys by making it possible to ascend to the skies. The vehicle will seat four people, and it will be able to take off vertically. Terrafugia, the American company who came up with the idea, hope to have the car in production by the end of the 2020s, when hybrid engine technology will have advanced enough to provide power for both road and air transportation.

Flying high

People have been dreaming of flying cars for decades. One of the first to get off the ground was the Aerocar, developed between the 1940s and 1960s. Its wings were detached and folded into a trailer for driving on roads.

Aerocar

The V-22 Osprey

The TF-X design uses technology pioneered by the V-22 Osprey military aircraft. The Osprey can tilt its rotors upward to take off like a helicopter, and then swing them forward to fly fast at subsonic speed, like a plane.

HOW IT WORKS

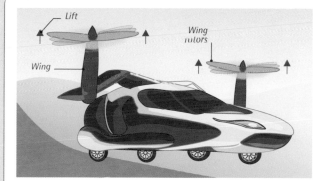

Lift

Wing rotors

Wing

To take off, no runway is needed. The wings fold out and the wing rotors point up, so the car's takeoff is close to vertical. Once airborne, the wing rotors rotate forward. The takeoff is completely automatic—the driver does not need to control it.

Tail fan

The cruising speed is 200 mph (320 kph) and the maximum journey length is 500 miles (800 km). During the cruise, the batteries that power the wheels and rotors are recharged by the spinning tail fan.

Like the takeoff, landing is automatic. The driver pre-selects a landing zone, and if the weather permits, the TF-X lands safely. The driver can take back control if the touchdown site is unsafe. If the engines all fail, a parachute deploys, preventing the craft from crashing.

The James Webb Space Telescope has a 21-ft (6.5-m) wide gold-coated mirror that is designed to pick up heat coming from the very edge of the universe. The mirror is shaded from the unwanted heat of the sun and Earth by a tennis-court-sized shield.

Secondary mirror reflects heat picked up by main mirror onto central camera

Layered heat shield reflects heat away from the mirror

Curved primary mirror made of 18 hexagonal units

Startracker orientates the spacecraft

Antenna for communication with Earth

Control systems are located in the spacecraft bus

SPACE TELESCOPE

>> At half the length of a 737 airliner, the James Webb Space Telescope (JWST) is the largest space telescope ever thought up. Due to launch in 2018, it is destined to search for the faint heat signatures coming from the very first stars and galaxies that formed after the Big Bang. The satellite is named after the NASA director who oversaw the Apollo missions that sent astronauts to the moon.

HOW IT WORKS

>> The JWST is so sensitive, it could detect the body heat of a bumblebee on the moon. The spacecraft is looking for heat, or infrared radiation, because that is all that is left of the light that shone from early stars. On their 13.6-billion-year journey to Earth, the visible light waves from these stars have been stretched and have become invisible heat waves.

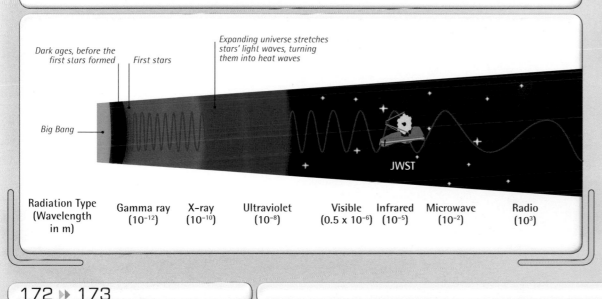

Dark ages, before the first stars formed

First stars

Expanding universe stretches stars' light waves, turning them into heat waves

Big Bang

JWST

Radiation Type (Wavelength in m)	Gamma ray (10^{-12})	X-ray (10^{-10})	Ultraviolet (10^{-8})	Visible (0.5×10^{-6})	Infrared (10^{-5})	Microwave (10^{-2})	Radio (10^{3})

Eye in space

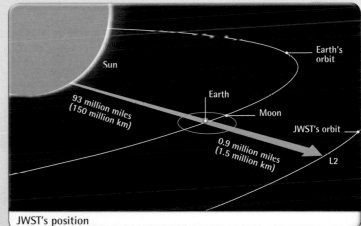

HST's mirror is made from polished glass.

JWST's mirror is made of beryllium coated in gold.

▲ The JWST will replace the Hubble Space Telescope (HST)—which launched in 1990—as the largest mirror working in space. The larger the mirror, the more things it can see, and the JWST's mirror is seven times larger than that of the HST. It is so large that, for it to fit inside a rocket, it has to be made from hexagonal segments that will fold out after reaching orbit.

Sun

93 million miles (150 million km)

Earth

Moon

Earth's orbit

JWST's orbit

0.9 million miles (1.5 million km)

L2

JWST's position

▲ The JWST needs to work somewhere very dark and cold. It will take up the position beyond Earth called L2. The gravity of Earth and the sun will work together to swing the JWST around the sun at the same pace as Earth, meaning it will always be shielded from the hot, bright glare of the sun by Earth.

Completely isolated

The D-Wave computer is housed in this special room. Inside is a near perfect vacuum, while the walls shield the processor from Earth's magnetism. A powerful refrigeration system cools the computer to −459°F (−273°C)—considerably colder than outer space!

The D-Wave room has 15 layers of shielding

▶▶ D-Wave

This thumbnail-sized chip is the processor for the D-Wave quantum computer. It is not made of silicon, but from superconducting niobium wires. It contains 1,000 quantum bits, or qubits, which can work 100 million times faster than a classical computer chip.

QUANTUM COMPUTER

Superconductors are materials that, when chilled to very low temperatures, allow electricity to pass easily through them—and they could help bring about a revolution in how computers store information. Computers that make use of superconductors are called quantum computers, and the D-Wave 2X is one such machine. A 32-bit classical computer handles 32 bits of information at a time; however, a 32-quantum bit, or qubit, computer can handle 4,294,967,296 bits all at once, greatly increasing what computers can do and how fast they can do it.

After silicon

Silicon electronics work by creating tiny gaps that block electric currents. To cram more electronics on to a microchip, those gaps must get smaller. However, if they get too small, they stop working. Designers are exploring new ways of processing information. One option is to use photonic circuits that use pulses of light, not electricity, to transmit information.

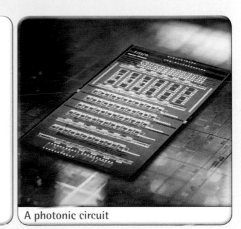
A photonic circuit

HOW IT WORKS

A traditional computer processor is a set of billions of switches. These are represented as a code of 1s (for on) and 0s (for off). Quantum computers get their processing power from storing information on a subatomic particle. When we measure a characteristic of a particle, it can represent a 1 or a 0. However, before we measure it, quantum effects mean the particle is both on and off, both 0 and 1, at the same time. This unknown state means it is a quantum bit, or qubit.

On   Off

A bit, short for "binary unit," can have one of two states: 1 or 0. It is impossible for it to be anything in between.

This point is neither 1 nor 0, but a combination of the two.

A 1 or a 0 can be represented by a characteristic of a particle such as an atom or electron. But quantum physics has shown that these particles can have two characteristics, meaning they'd represent 0 and 1 at the same time.

Every point can be expressed as two numbers, which are the probability of it being 0 or 1.

70%

30%

It is possible to calculate the chance of the qubit being 0 and the chance of it being 1, and so one qubit contains two bits of information.

▲ **Ripples in space**

In 1916, German scientist Albert Einstein predicted that massive accelerating objects produce gravity waves that ripple through space and time. The waves detected in 2016 were made by two black holes colliding 1.3 billion light-years away from Earth.

GRAVITY WAVES

In early 2016, a team of scientists belonging to the Laser Interferometer Gravitational-Wave Observatory (LIGO) in the United States held a press conference to make an important announcement. They had made a discovery that may be one of the most remarkable and important scientific breakthroughs of the past hundred years: They had made the first-ever direct detection of ripples in space and time called gravity waves.

HOW IT WORKS

The instrument that detected the gravity waves used laser beams to detect tiny changes in the distance between mirrors caused by gravity waves. The instrument is so sensitive that it can detect a change of one-thousandth the width of an atomic nucleus over its 2-mile (4-km) length.

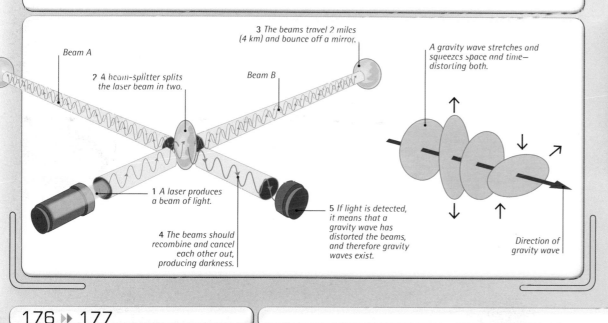

Beam A

2 A beam-splitter splits the laser beam in two.

Beam B

3 The beams travel 2 miles (4 km) and bounce off a mirror.

A gravity wave stretches and squeezes space and time—distorting both.

1 A laser produces a beam of light.

4 The beams should recombine and cancel each other out, producing darkness.

5 If light is detected, it means that a gravity wave has distorted the beams, and therefore gravity waves exist.

Direction of gravity wave

New knowledge

A supernova produces X-rays

Every time scientists found a new way to look at the universe—in visible light, and then at radio wavelengths, X-rays, and so on—they made new discoveries. Gravity waves give them yet another new way to look at the universe.

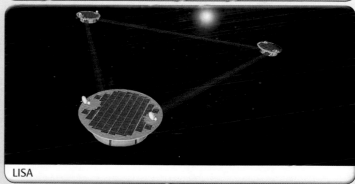

LISA

There are plans to launch a gravity-wave detector called LISA (Laser Interferometric Space Antenna) in 2034. Three spacecraft 3 million miles (5 million km) apart will bounce laser beams between them and search for gravity waves.

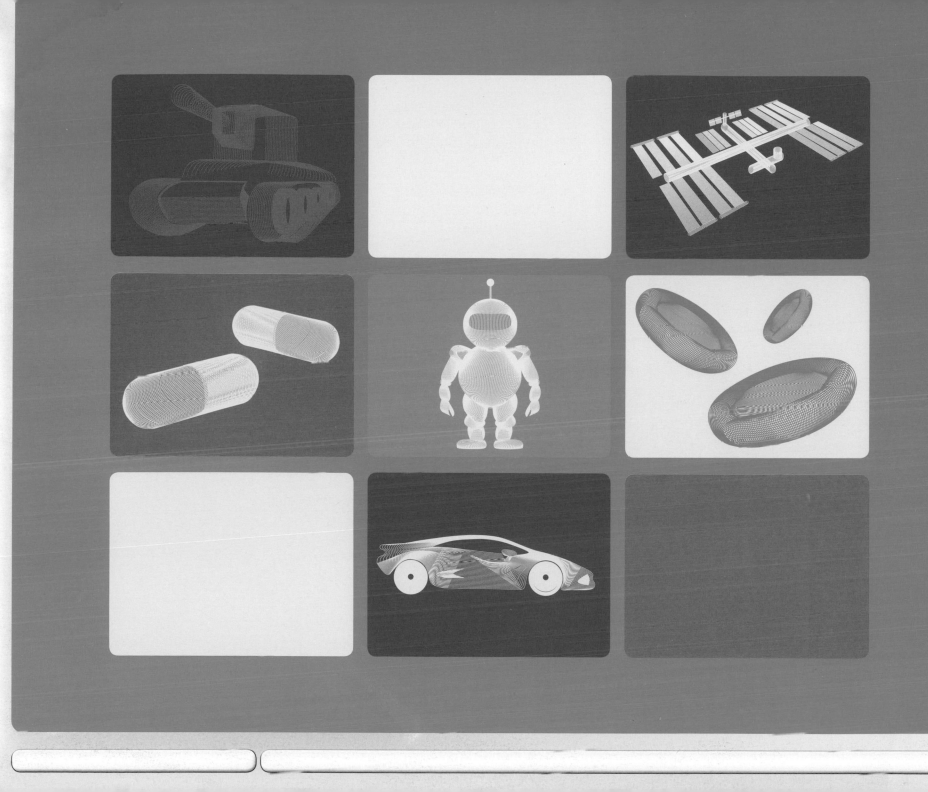

WHAT'S NEXT?

⌃ TRANSPORTATION

Transportation will probably develop in three ways: super-fast vehicles for carrying people who can't wait, more spacious and comfortable transportation for the masses, and large robotic cargo vehicles for hauling goods all around the world.

- ◀ Electric and hydrogen-fueled vehicles will become more popular than vehicles running on fossil fuels.
- ◀ Self-driving cars and trucks will make road transportation safer.
- ◀ Airliners using the latest scientific research will jet people around the globe faster than the speed of sound.
- ◀ Hypersonic (more than five times faster than the speed of sound) aircraft will make it possible to fly halfway around the world in only a couple of hours.

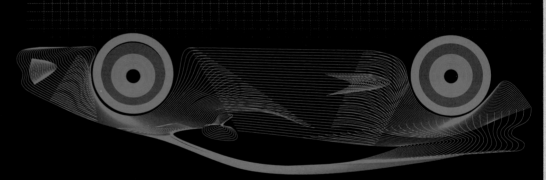

⌃ MILITARY

The Internet, GPS, radar, jet engines, and computers all had their origins in military research, and the military will continue to be a major driver of innovation and invention.

- ◀ Unmanned Combat Air Vehicles (UCAVs) will replace manned attack planes and autonomous robots, and remotely controlled vehicles will become commonplace.
- ◀ Stealth technology and conventional camouflage will be enhanced by increasingly effective invisibility systems.
- ◀ Governments around the world will spend more time and money on securing their countries against attacks on their national security from the Internet.

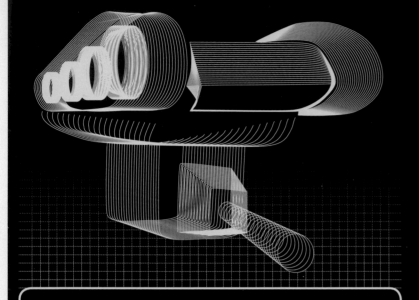

ENERGY

Increasing global energy demands will drive improvements in existing sources of energy and the development of new energy sources. Environmental concerns mean that new energy technologies will have to be clean and green.

▶ After decades of research, the first nuclear power stations based on atomic fusion will be built.
▶ Airborne wind turbines tethered to the ground will generate electricity from high-speed, high-altitude winds.
▶ Countries with access to the ocean will extract hydrogen from seawater and use it as a fuel for electricity generation and transportation.
▶ Solar power satellites may be launched to capture solar energy and beam it down to Earth.

SPACE

Following the first manned landing on Mars in the 2030s, space agencies begin to plan for their next manned landing—possibly on one of Jupiter's moons. Meanwhile, private companies will continue to exploit near-Earth space.

▶ The first privately funded space station will receive its first guests for a vacation in orbit.
▶ A new Space Race to establish the first permanently manned Moonbase will be contested between the United States and China.
▶ A space probe will land on Jupiter's moon Europa and bore down through the surface ice into the ocean below to search for life.
▶ Space telescopes may observe a planet that appears to exhibit signs of intelligent life, including radio transmissions, and a debris field that may be the remains of rockets and spacecraft.
▶ Scientists may begin transforming Mars to prepare for the day when human settlers start moving there.

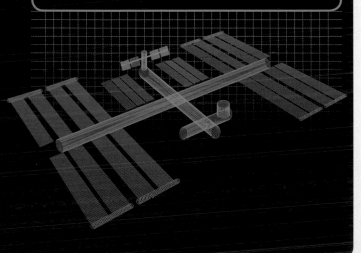

COMMUNICATIONS

Communications encompass everything from newspapers and broadcasting to broadband and telephones—and all will be transformed by future technologies.

▶ Smartphones will not remain as stand-alone handsets for much longer; they are likely to be built into all sorts of other devices.
▶ Traditional news organizations may cease to exist; instead, they will be replaced by individuals posting reports, eyewitness accounts, and opinions pieces online on their own video channels.
▶ In a few decades, personal computers will be as powerful as today's supercomputers.
▶ Television will be broadcast in UDTV (Ultra-high Definition TV), with 16 times the definition of television today.

▶ What's next?

NANOTECHNOLOGY

Tiny technologies will find applications throughout all sorts of industries, including manufacturing, agriculture, electronics, energy, and healthcare. Materials created to order, atom by atom, will be tailored to the precise properties needed for each application.

▶ Nanotech coatings on buildings and bridges will neutralize air pollution.
▶ Diamond-like materials 50 times stronger than steel will be developed by nanotechnology.
▶ Nanobots the size of blood cells will be injected into the human body to repair damage, or to seek out invaders such as viruses, bacteria, and cancer cells.
▶ Shrinking nanotechnology even further to smaller scales called picotechnology and femtotechnology will be used to manipulate matter at the atomic and subatomic scale.

ROBOTICS

Robots will become an increasingly common feature of our lives. More capable, internet-linked robots with more advanced artificial intelligence will work alongside human workers in business and industry. Labor-saving robotic devices will become more common in our homes.

▶ As artificial intelligence improves, robots will be able to do an increasing number of jobs, and potentially do them better than humans.
▶ Japan, the world leader in robot technology, will send humanoid robots into space in place of astronauts.
▶ Robots will begin to replace guide dogs to guide blind people and assist people with other disabilities.

BIOTECHNOLOGY

Biotechnology, the combination of living organisms and technology to solve problems and make commercial products, is expected to have a far-reaching impact on four fields in particular: medicine, agriculture, industry, and the environment.

▶ Genetically improved photosynthesis will increase crop yields to help feed the growing global population.
▶ Sensors built from genetically engineered living cells will be implanted in the human body to collect medical data.
▶ Solar panels will be grown from living plant cells.
▶ Super-fast computer memory devices will be made from naturally magnetic bacteria.
▶ Bacteria will be employed to clean up pollution.

HEALTH AND MEDICINE

Advances in genetics and biotechnology may finally reveal mechanisms for curing cancer and Alzheimer's Disease, and for repairing damage to spinal cords, eyes, and brains. The cell damage that causes the effects of aging may be reversible, too.

▸▸ It will become possible to upload a human mind to a supercomputer.
▸▸ The Internet of DNA may become a reality, enabling researchers to access the genomes of thousands of people online, to increase their ability to find cures for common illnesses.
▸▸ New body parts and even whole organs will be made by 3-D bio-printing, printing layer upon layer of living cells.
▸▸ Survival rates for many cancers will reach almost 100 percent thanks to advances in medical knowledge made possible by technology.
▸▸ The cost of expensive drugs will fall when they are mass-produced using genetically engineered organisms instead of making them chemically.

EVERYDAY LIFE

Technology will continue to subtly affect our everyday lives, with many small advances such as faster Internet connections making new ways of working and learning possible.

▸▸ Schools may be phased out in favor of live streaming of lessons to children's homes.
▸▸ Car manufacturers will produce cars with a self-repairing coating on their bodywork.
▸▸ Internet and real-time translation programs will make it possible for people to communicate with each other, in any language, all over the world.
▸▸ Coins and paper money will finally disappear, fully replaced by digital payment methods.

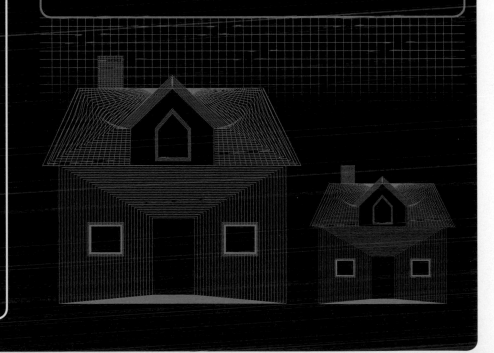

GLOSSARY

3

3-D printer
A computer-controlled printing machine that can produce a three-dimensional object by printing layer upon layer of plastic or another material.

activity tracker
An electronic device that senses the wearer's movements and records them for analysis, often by using an app on a smartphone or computer.

air resistance
A force that tries to slow objects down when they move through air. Also known as drag.

altitude
The height of an object or point above sea level or the ground.

artificial intelligence
A branch of computer science concerned with developing computer systems that simulate human learning and decision-making.

atom
The smallest possible particle of a chemical element. Atoms are the basic building blocks of matter. They join together to form molecules. Each atom is made of even smaller particles called subatomic particles. The nucleus at the center contains protons and neutrons, and these are surrounded by electrons.

cell
The smallest unit of a living organism, and the building blocks of plants and animals. Also, a cell is one of the electricity-generating units within a battery.

cerebral palsy
An illness that involves impaired muscle coordination typically caused by damage to the brain before or just after birth.

chip
A set of tiny electronic circuits mounted on a single piece of semiconducting material, usually silicon. One chip can hold up to several billion switches, called transistors. There are different types of chips. Memory chips store data. Microprocessors contain a computer's central processing unit (CPU).

circuit
An unbroken path that allows electricity to flow along it.

collaborative robot
A robot designed to work with human workers in a shared workspace.

computer
An electronic machine that processes information according to sets of instructions called programs. Computers have a way of receiving information (input), somewhere to store information (memory), a part that processes information (the central processing unit, or processor), and a way to display information (output).

G

G-force
A force produced by acceleration and measured by comparing it to the force of gravity at the Earth's surface, which is 1G.

GPS
Global Positioning System. A network of satellites orbiting Earth, transmitting radio signals to receivers on Earth that use the signals to calculate their position. GPS is the basis of satellite navigation.

graphene
An ultrathin honeycomb structure of carbon that is stronger than steel.

gravity
A force of attraction between any two masses in the universe. All masses have their own force of gravity, but the effect is usually noticeable only for the most massive objects such as stars, planets, and moons.

gravity waves
Ripples in space-time produced by intense gravitational forces, predicted in 1916 and finally observed in 2016.

gyroscope
A wheel that is able to spin around an axis that is itself free to move. Gyroscopes are used in cell phones to determine the positioning of the phone.

J

jet engine
A type of internal combustion engine in which fuel is burned in air to create a jet of fast-moving gas to propel an aircraft or other vehicle.

K

kinetic energy
The energy that something has because it is moving.

L

Large Hadron Collider
The world's biggest and most powerful subatomic particle collider, designed to accelerate two beams of protons to almost the speed of light, and then smash them into each other to test the predictions of scientific theories.

LCD
Liquid Crystal Display. LCDs use electric currents to make tiny crystals appear light or dark to form letters or images on a screen.

LED
Light-emitting diode. A small electronic component that glows when an electric current flows through it.

Internet of Things
The network of everyday objects, such as cars, kitchen appliances, medical implants, and buildings, that contain embedded Internet-connected devices.

ion
An atom or molecule that has gained or lost one or more electrons and, as a result, has an electric charge.

atomic fusion
A chemical reaction where two or more atomic nuclei collide to become a new nucleus. This process releases a lot of energy.

augmented reality
A view of the real world supplemented with computer-generated information.

autonomous
A device or system that is capable of completing a complex task by itself.

battery
A device that stores chemical energy and can be used to convert that energy into electrical energy. When a battery is connected to a closed path called a circuit, electric current flows from one end of the battery through the circuit and back to the other end of the battery.

Big Bang
The event that is thought to mark the birth of our universe approximately 13.7 billion years ago.

Bluetooth
A standard method for exchanging data between devices by a wireless (radio) link over short distances.

catalyst
A substance that speeds up the rate of a chemical reaction, but does not itself change in the process.

dark matter
An unknown physical substance that is thought to form about five-sixths of the matter in the universe.

downdraft
A downward-flowing current of air. The air blown downward by a helicopter or other rotorcraft is an example of downdraft.

drone
A remotely controlled pilotless aircraft.

electronic ink
Material that responds to electrical impulses by changing its appearance to create text and images on a screen.

energy
The capacity to do work. Energy cannot be created or destroyed, but it can be converted from one form to another. Every activity in the universe involves the conversion of energy.

ethylene tetrafluoroethylene
A type of plastic, also known as ETFE, that is strong and corrosion-resistant over a wide temperature range. ETFE sheeting is used for roofing and cladding in the construction industry.

friction
A force between two surfaces that are in contact. It tends to resist them sliding past each other.

hard disk
The place where a computer's files are stored.

heat
A form of energy, also known as thermal energy, that is stored in a substance as vibrations of its atoms or molecules.

Higgs boson
The subatomic particle responsible for matter having mass. It was observed by experiments carried out by the Large Hadron Collider in 2012.

hydraulic
Operated by the movement of a liquid (usually oil) under pressure.

Hyperloop
A proposed high-speed transportation system that relies on pressurized capsules being propelled through a closed tube.

inertia
The tendency of a physical object to resist any change to its state of motion.

information technology
The use of computers, networks, and communication technology to store, process, and transmit data.

insulation
Material that reduces or prevents the loss of sound, heat, or electric current.

lift
An upward force on an aircraft wing caused by the movement of air around it.

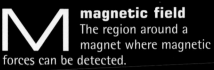

magnetic field
The region around a magnet where magnetic forces can be detected.

maglev
A transportation system that uses magnetic levitation for support and propulsion. A strong magnetic field lifts the vehicle above its track and propels it along.

mass
The amount of matter in something.

microprocessor
The main chip in a computer that contains the computer's central processing unit (CPU) and carries out the instructions of a computer program. Also known as a processor.

miniaturization
Reducing something in size. Usually used to refer to the trend of computer chips becoming smaller and more powerful.

motherboard
The main circuit board of a computer or other electric device.

nanotube
A tiny cylinder, visible only under a microscope, that strengthens a material.

neutrino
An elementary particle with zero electric charge and almost no mass.

niobium
A silver-gray metal used in superconducting materials.

OLED
Organic light-emitting diode. An LED in which the light-emitting substance is a carbon-based organic compound.

organic
Relating to materials that are made of carbon.

payload
The passengers or cargo carried by a vehicle, especially satellites or other space hardware, launched by a rocket.

photon
The zero-mass elementary particle of electromagnetic radiation, including visible light. Like all elementary particles, it also exhibits wavelike properties.

pixel
A tiny colored dot that forms the smallest part of a picture on a display such as a television or computer screen.

potential energy
One of several forms of energy that something has because of its position or state. For example, a stretched rubber band has elastic potential energy.

processor
The main chip in a computer that contains the computer's central processing unit (CPU) and carries out the instructions of a computer program. Also known as a microprocessor.

proton
A subatomic particle with a positive electric charge, found in the nucleus of an atom.

prototype
An early version of a product or part, built for testing or demonstration purposes before large-scale production begins.

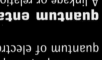

quantum
The smallest unit of any form of energy. For example, the photon is the quantum of electromagnetic energy.

quantum entanglement
A linkage or relationship between two particles such that the quantum state of one determines the quantum state of the other, even if they are separated in space.

quark
A subatomic particle found inside larger particles (called hadrons), such as the proton and neutron.

recycling
Reusing materials and products that would otherwise be thrown away as garbage.

RFID
Radio-frequency identification. Method for tracking things by using electronic tags that respond to radio signals.

robot
A computer-controlled machine capable of carrying out some or all of its actions autonomously.

rocket core
The central stage of a multistage rocket to which booster rockets may be attached.

rotor
A rotating part of a machine. The rotating part of an electric motor and a helicopter's spinning blades are examples of rotors.

SEM
Scanning electron microscope. A type of electron microscope that produces images of a sample magnified up to about 500,000 times by scanning it with a beam of electrons.

smart TV
A television set that can be connected to the Internet to access extra services.

stack effect
The movement of air into, through, and out of buildings due to the buoyancy of warm air compared to cooler air. Also known as the chimney effect.

Space Race
Rivalry between the United States and the Soviet Union (USSR) in space exploration in the 1960s, with the aim of landing astronauts on the moon.

stealth
Any technology designed to make detection difficult to detect, especially by sight or radar.

subatomic particle
A particle that is smaller than an atom. Protons, neutrons, electrons, and quarks are examples of subatomic particles.

sync
Short for synchronize, and means making processes or data in different devices match by copying information from one device to another.

turbine
A device with blades that rotate when a liquid or gas flows through it, converting the kinetic energy of the liquid or gas into rotary motion and electrical energy.

virtual reality
An environment created by a computer to simulate part of the real world or an invented world, with which a user can interact.

weight
A force produced by gravity acting on an object's mass. While mass remains constant, weight depends on the local force of gravity.

Wi-Fi
A short-range wireless (radio) technology that is used to connect electronic devices to computer networks such as the Internet.

wireless
A description of technology that transfers information between devices that are not connected to each other by wires or any other physical link.

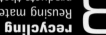
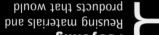

INDEX

ACKNOWLEDGMENTS

DK would like to thank:
Victoria Pyke for proofreading; Carron Brown for the index; Meenal Goel, Rashika Kachroo, Roshni Kapur for design assistance; Ann Baggaley, Sreshtha Bhattacharya, Agnibesh Das, Sarah Isle, Priyanka Kharbanda, Ashwin Khurana, Deeksha Miglani, and Sonia Yooshing for editorial assistance.

All technologies, names, and designs are protected by copyright and trademark.

Special thanks to all of the manufacturers, design and architectural studios, and photographers who answered numerous queries and gave permission to use their images throughout the book.

Key: a-above, b-below, c-center, l-left, r-right, t-top

2 123RF.com: Sebastian Kaulitzki (tr). Artiphon, Inc.. Courtesy of Whill: (crb). EHANG, Inc.: (clb). Getty Images: Lionel Flusin (tl); Image By Steve Passlow (br). Gewers Pudewill: (ca). Omer Hacıomeroglu: (cb). 2-191 iStockphoto.com: fazon1 (Background). 4 reactable.com: (bl). Rolls-Royce plc: (cla). 5 Getty Images: Lionel Flusin (tl). Joseph Viker: (bl). 6 Courtesy of D*Haus: (bl). Courtesy of International Business Machines Corporation: (tl). 7 Terrafugia/www.terrafugia.com: (cla). 9 Getty Images: Image By Steve Passlow (cr). Courtesy of Gopro: (cl). © 2016 Hello Games Limited: No Man's Sky is a trade mark of Hello Games Limited (bl). Used with permission from Microsoft. ROLI.com: (bc). SHARP corporation: (tc). 10 Used with permission from Microsoft: (bl). 11 Used with permission from Microsoft: (tl, c). U.S. Air Force: Airman 1st Class Anthony Jennings (cb). 12 Courtesy of Gopro: (cra). Samuel Twist. 13 Courtesy of Gopro: (br). LSST Corporation: Todd Mason, Mason Productions Inc. (tr). Rex by Shutterstock: KeystoneUSA-ZUMA (cla). 14 IHS Technology: (c). iStockphoto.com: Stratol (bc). 15 Used with permission from Microsoft: (All images). 16 Courtesy the artist and Bethanie Brady Artist Management. 17 Courtesy of Apple Inc.: (tl, cr). 18 3Doodler. 19 Bocusini by Print2Taste: (tl). 20 3Dvarius: Laurent Bernadac (tr); Thomas Tetu (br). ROLI.com: (tl). 21 Doppler Labs: (cla, clb). reactable.com: (br). Yamaha Music Europe GmbH (UK), Pro Music Department: (tc). 22-23 IHS Technology: (tc). 22 Courtesy of Apple Inc.: (bc/5 images bottom of page). 23 Getty Images: Yoshikazu Tsuno (bc). 24 IHS Technology: (tc, bc). 25 © 2016 Hello Games Limited: No Man's Sky is a trade mark of Hello Games Limited (tr). Sony Computer Entertainment UK Limited: (crb). 26 123RF.com: Mariusz Blach (ca). Corbis: Fotofeeling / Westend61 (cb). LG Electronics. 27 Getty Images: Jung Yeon-Je (crb). 28 Artiphon, Inc.: (All images). 29 Artiphon, Inc.: (br). Getty Images: Sovfoto (tr). Noisy Jelly: (tl). 30 Getty Images: Andrzej Wojcicki / Science Photo Library. 31 NASA: Emmett Given (br). 32 Corbis: Albert Pena / Icon Sportswire. 33 Dreamstime.com: Norgal (cla). 34 elemental path: CogniToys Dino (tl). Mattel, Inc.: © 2016 Mattel, Inc. All Rights Reserved (br). 35 Courtesy of Osmo: (tl). SHARP corporation: (crb, tr). Wondernik: (bl, br). 36 Used with permission from Microsoft: (All images). 37 Alamy Stock Photo: Interfoto (tl). Science Photo Library: Manfred Kage (cla). 38 Getty Images: Image By Steve Passlow. 39 Alamy Stock Photo: Stocktrek Images, Inc. (cl). 41 ElliptiGO Inc.: (br). Hybrid Air Vehicles Ltd.: (bl). Jetman Dubai: (c). Nick Kaloterakis: (tc). Rolls-Royce plc: (cr). Volocopter: e-volo

GmbH (bc). Wessex Water/Julian James photography: (tl). 42 Lexus: (tl); Courtesy of Lexus Division (UK). 43 Alamy Stock Photo: Henry Westheim Photography (tl); Stan Rohrer (ca). Lexus: (cb). 44 Nick Kaloterakis: (tr). SpaceX. 45 Blue Origin: (br). 46 Courtesy of Whill: (tr). 47 Courtesy of Scalevo: (tc). Courtesy of Whill: (ca, cb, bc). 48-49 Tesla Motors: (All images). 50 Courtesy Virgin Galactic. 51 Corbis: Sergei Chirikov / epa (cl). 52 Wessex Water/Julian James photography. 53 Amager Resource Center: (tr). Science Photo Library: Pascal Goetgheluck (tl). 54 ElliptiGO Inc.. 55 Reuters: Baz Ratner (cla). 56 NASA: (tl); Robert Markowitz. 57 ESA: NASA (ca). NASA: (tr, cr); MSFC (bc). 58 Hybrid Air Vehicles Ltd.. 59 Corbis: John Lund / Blend Images (cl). 60-61 Jetman Dubai: jetman.com (All images). 62 Courtesy of Superpedestrian: Michael D Spencer (tl). DFKI GmbH: (br). 63 iStockphoto.com: Joe_Potato (r). Nike: (cl). Courtesy of WaterCar: (bc); www.WaterCar.com (bl). 64 Airbus-image exm company: Hervé Goussé (tl). Olivier Cabaret. 65 Dreamstime.com: Travis Fisher (tr). NASA: Lockheed Martin Corporation (tl). 66 Rolls-Royce plc: (tc). 67 Used with permission of Royal Caribbean Cruises Ltd.: (tc). 68 NASA: Goddard Space Flight Center. 69 NASA: JHUAPL / SwRI (cla). 70 Dreamstime.com: Phanuwatn (background). Volocopter: e-volo GmbH. 71 Volocopter: e-volo GmbH (tl). 73 Alamy Stock Photo: 68images.com - Axel Schmies (tr). Corbis: Catherine Bassetti (bl). Getty Images: Kimberley Coole (cr). ICEHOTEL, Jukkasjärvi: Christopher Hauser (bc). The Solomon R. Guggenheim Museum, New York: David Heald © SRGF, NY. (c). Joseph Viker: (tl). 74-75 Alamy Stock Photo: 68images.com - Axel Schmies. 74 Getty Images: Chris Jackson (cb). Rex by Shutterstock: MC Films (crb). Imre Solt: (bc). 76 Adam Mork Architectural Photography. 77 3XN Architects: (tr). Adam Mork Architectural Photography: (bc, br, cb). 78 ICEHOTEL, Jukkasjärvi: Christopher Hauser. 79 Getty Images: Jonathan Nackstrand (tl). ICEHOTEL, Jukkasjärvi: Paulina Holmgren (tc); Martin Smedsén (cl); Asaf Kliger (cr). 80 Joseph Viker. 81 Alamy Stock Photo: blickwinkel (tl). Foster + Partners: (br). 82 Alamy Stock Photo: Photos 12. 83 123RF.com: lachris77 (tr). Alamy Stock Photo: Agencja Fotograficzna Caro (c); Nina Reistad (tr). Corbis: Yann Arthus-Bertrand (tl). Dreamstime.com: Patricia Hofmeester (br); Francisco Javier Gil Oreja (cra). Robert Harding Picture Library: Christian Reister (crb). 84 Heatherwick Studio Rolling Bridge: Steve Speller (crb). National Arboretum, Canberra: John Gollings (tl). 85 Corbis: Charles Pertwee (br). Images by NLÉ: (clb). Nextoffice: Parham Taghioff (tr). 86 McDowell+Benedetti (architect), Alan Baxter Associates (structural engineer) and Qualter Hall (M&E designer and contractor): Timothy Soar (All images). 87 Dreamstime.com: Ronniechua (cr). Getty Images: Barcroft (tc). 88 Latitude Image: Nicolas Chorier. 89 Dreamstime.com: Paul Prescott (tr). Getty Images: Kimberley Coole (tl). 90 The Solomon R. Guggenheim Museum, New York: David Heald © SRGF, NY.. 91 Alamy Stock Photo: Russell Kord (tl). Art on Track: (tr). The Tate Modern: © Tate, London 2016 (ca). 92 Gewers Pudewill: (br). 93 Rendering of + POOL. Design by Family & PlayLab. www.pluspool.org: (cl). 94 Courtesy of Nakheel. Alexander Heilner: (cla). 95 NASA: (cla). 96 Corbis: Catherine Bassetti (r). 97 Corbis: Catherine Bassetti (tl). Washington State Department of Transportation: (c). 98 123RF.com: Sebastian Kaulitzki (tc). TU Delft: Renee Mors, Delft University of Technology (cr, br). 99 Jens Bauer/KIT: (br). Copyright 2016 HRL Laboratories: Dan Little Photography (t).

Wyss Institute at Harvard University: (cl). 101 © CERN: Maximilien Brice (bl). Corbis: Cheng Min / Xinhua Press (tl); Jan Woitas / dpa (tc); Patrick Pleul / dpa (br). Courtesy of Ekso Bionics: (c). Hackaball Ltd: (cr). Volvo Car Uk Ltd: (tr). 102-103 Tesla Motors: (All images). 104 Ken Richardson Photography: (c, cl/eyes). 105 Corbis: Jan Woitas / dpa (cb). Ken Richardson Photography: (tl, c). 106 raspberrypi.org: (tl). 107 Corbis: Frank Duenzl / dpa (cra). Hackaball Ltd: (crb). 108 Corbis: Patrick Pleul / dpa. 109 Caterpillar Inc.: (bc). 110-111 Courtesy of Ekso Bionics. 110 Courtesy of Ekso Bionics: (bc). 111 naturepl.com: John Abbott (bc). 112 © CERN: Maximilien Brice. 113 Getty Images: Lionel Flusin (ftr). Science Photo Library: Cern (tc); Claudia Marcelloni, CERN (tr). 114 GoSun Stove: (tr, br). Volvo Car Uk Ltd: (tl). 115 Columbia University's Engineering School: Konkuk University, Korea Research Institute of Standards and Science, Seoul National University (cr). Revolights: (tl). Kyuho Song: (bl, bc). 116 Kenedy & Violich Architecture, Ltd. 117 Kenedy & Violich Architecture, Ltd: (c, br). SolarWindow Technologies, Inc.: (tc). 118 Rolls-Royce plc. 119 BAE Systems 2007: (bc). Rolls-Royce plc: (cra). 120 Corbis: Cheng Min / Xinhua Press. 121 Corbis: Xiao Yijiu / Xinhua Press (cl). 123 Corbis: KTSDESIGN / Science Photo Library (c); Science Picture Co. (tl). Courtesy of D*Haus: (bl). Getty Images: Science Photo Library - SCIEPRO (cr). Omer Hacıomeroglu: (br). NASA: JPL-Caltech (cl). Panono: (tc, tc/Camera). 124 Omer Hacıomeroglu: (cra). 125 Courtesy of U.S. Navy: Mass Communication Specialist Seaman Chelsea Kennedy (crb). 126 Courtesy of Cleverpet. 127 WÜF, getwuf.com: (tl). 128 Courtesy of D*Haus. 129 Reuters: (c). 130 Fontus: (bl). 131 Fontus: (cr). pAge Drinking Paper: Luke Hydrick (cl). 132 Science Photo Library: Steve Gschmeissner. 133 Amazon.com, Inc.: (tl). 134 Alamy Stock Photo: Vladislav Ociacia. 135 Össur UK: (t, cb, br). 136 PrecisionHawk. 137 Getty Images: Cessna Citation Jet / AFP (tl). PrecisionHawk: (tr, cra, crb, br). 138 Garmin: (br). 139 EMBR labs: Niccolo Casas (cl). 140 Panono: (tr). 141 Science Photo Library: Andy Crump (cla). 142 Foster + Partners. Getty Images: Stocktrek Images (bl). NASA: (clb). 143 NASA: (cla). 144 Second Sight Medical Products: (cra). 145 Corbis: Science Picture Co. (cla). Second Sight Medical Products: (r). 146 Getty Images: Paul Kennedy (bl). TheOceanCleanup.com. 149 NASA: (tl, tc, c, cr, br). 150 Corbis: KTSDESIGN / Science Photo Library (cla). Courtesy of MC10 Inc.: (br). 151 Corbis: VOISIN / PHANIE / phanie / Phanie Sarl (cl). Getty Images: Science Photo Library - SCIEPRO (tr). Seoul National University: Dae-Hyeong Kim (br). 153 Hyperloop Transportation Technologies: (bc). Courtesy of International Business Machines Corporation: (cl). Science Photo Library: Christian Darkin (tl). Terrafugia/www.terrafugia.com: (tl). University of Rochester: J. Adam Fenster (br). 154 Phonebloks. 155 Corbis: Ritchie B. Tongo (br). Phonebloks: (cr). 156 EHANG, Inc.. 157 EHANG, Inc.: (tr). Foster + Partners: (bc). 158 University of Rochester: J. Adam Fenster. 159 U.S. Air Force: Staff Sgt Jeremy M. Wilson (c). 160 NASA: (br). Science Photo Library: Martin Marietta Corporation (tc). 161 Dreamstime.com: Peter Jurik (tl). NASA: (br). SpaceWorks Enterprises, Inc.: (tr). 162 Hyperloop Transportation Technologies. 164 Dorling Kindersley: Jamie Marshall (tl/Street). Dreamstime.com: Brian Sedgbeer. Science Photo Library: Christian Darkin (tl, crb). 165 Corbis: Hero Images (tr). Science Photo Library: Richard Kail (tl). 166 123RF.com: Valerijs Kostreckis. 168 Alamy Stock Photo: Blend Images (cr, tl, tr); Design Pics Inc (b, cla, ca). 170 Terrafugia/

www.terrafugia.com: (br). 171 Corbis: (tl); Ed Darack / Science Faction (cla). 172 NASA: Northrop Grumman. 173 NASA: (tl). 174 NASA: Quantum Artificial Intelligence Laboratory (tc). © D-Wave Systems Inc. All rights reserved.. 175 Courtesy of International Business Machines Corporation: (tl). 177 NASA: (tr). Science Photo Library: Mark Garlick (tl). 191 Alamy Stock Photo: blickwinkel (cla). Columbia University's Engineering School: Konkuk University, Korea Research Institute of Standards and Science, Seoul National University (bc). Corbis: John Lund / Blend Images (br). DFKI GmbH: (tc). NASA: Lockheed Martin Corporation (cra). Science Photo Library: Claudia Marcelloni, CERN (tl). The Solomon R. Guggenheim Museum, New York: David Heald © SRGF, NY. (clb). Courtesy Virgin Galactic: (cb)